Instructor's Manual

STRUCTURE AND MEANING:
AN INTRODUCTION TO LITERATURE

Second Edition

Anthony Dubé

J. Karl Franson
University of Maine at Farmington

Russell E. Murphy
University of Arkansas at Little Rock

James W. Parins
University of Arkansas at Little Rock

HOUGHTON MIFFLIN COMPANY   BOSTON

Dallas   Geneva, Illinois
Hopewell, New Jersey   Palo Alto   London

Printed in the U.S.A.

ISBN: 0-395-32571-4

CONTENTS

Preface   v

FICTION

Chapter 1   Plot   2

Chapter 2   Character   7

Chapter 3   Point of View   13

Chapter 4   Theme or Meaning   20

Chapter 5   Style   25

Chapter 6   Other Stories to Read   30

Chapter 7   Heart of Darkness   34

POETRY

Introduction   38

Chapter 8   Denotation and Connotation   40

Chapter 9   Imagery   47

Chapter 10   Figurative Language   52

Chapter 11   Rhythm and Meter   57

Chapter 12   Sound Devices and Stanza Patterns   63

Chapter 13   Allusion and Symbol   69

Chapter 14   The Scheme of Meaning   80

Chapter 15   Other Poems to Read   91

DRAMA

Chapter 16   Plot   110

Chapter 17   Character   113

Chapter 18   Theme or Meaning   117

Chapter 19   Dramatic Language   119

Chapter 20   Other Plays to Read   122

PREFACE

Structure and Meaning contains many aids for the student; this Instructor's Manual aims to help the instructor by providing answers to exercise questions in the text. The answers, of course, cannot be exhaustive or proffer the one "correct" viewpoint. Quite the contrary, they are intended to be merely suggestive and to offer thought for lectures, discussions, and examinations.

We will be amply rewarded for our efforts if the manual furnishes the instructor with a convenient beginning and saves valuable time.

Anthony Dubé
J. Karl Franson
Russell E. Murphy
James W. Parins

FICTION

James Thurber

THE CATBIRD SEAT

1. a. Martin, conducting the trial of Mrs. Barrows, charges her with harassment and trying to destroy the efficiency of F & S, which also threatens his security.

   b. At Mrs. Barrows's apartment Martin is unable to find a suitable murder weapon; he drinks, smokes, admits to taking heroin, and threatens to kill Fitweiler.

   c. Mrs. Barrows tells Fitweiler "all" about Martin's strange behavior.

   d. Fitweiler makes Martin aware of Mrs. Barrows's accusations; and, after concluding that Mrs. Barrows has a persecution complex, he dismisses her from his employ.

2. a. The quiet, cautious, ineffectual Martin is the protagonist.

   b. He is the character who controls the main action, coming to grips with his problem and making plans for the demise of his antagonist; it is through his eyes that we view the unfolding of the story; and at the end, it is he who sits in "the catbird seat" (sitting pretty), gloating over his triumph.

   c. His prize is "to rub out" Mrs. Barrows.

3. a. The aggressive, power-obsessed Mrs. Barrows is the antagonist.

   b. The conflict is between Martin and Mrs. Barrows or Martin and the system she represents. Martin, whose position at F & S has gained him a sense of belonging and importance, is menaced by Mrs. Barrows, whom Fitweiler has hired as an efficiency expert to overhaul his business.

   c. The conflict is internal when Martin lives in the "fantasy" world and external when he returns to the "real" world.

4. When Mrs. Barrows announces her plans to reorganize Martin's department, the conflict erupts.

5. a. Martin's inability to find a suitable murder weapon prevents him from carrying out his plans to murder Mrs. Barrows and temporarily blocks him from achieving his goal.

   b. Mrs. Barrows's disclosure to Fitweiler of the truth about Martin's behavior at her apartment endangers Martin's "catbird seat" position. For this brief moment Martin is vulnerable and stands a chance of losing the battle.

6. a. The climactic scene occurs when Fitweiler cross-examines Martin.

   b. At this point, the reader remains unsure of the outcome; the reader still asks, "Will Martin win or lose?"

7. a. Having outwitted Mrs. Barrows, Martin does achieve his goal.

   b. The point at which Fitweiler fires Mrs. Barrows provides the resolution.

8. Thurber may be suggesting that (1) there is a limit to how far a person can be pushed; (2) the individual is important in a system; or (3) the underdog can defeat the strong.

Bernard Malamud

THE MAGIC BARREL

1. Leo uses Salzman, the marriage broker, in his search for a bride; Leo dismisses Salzman, who has failed to provide a suitable bride; Salzman offers Leo "a first-class bride" in the person of Lily Hirschorn; Leo's encounter with Lily Hirschorn leads to self-discovery; in a packet left by Salzman, Leo finds the picture of a girl who excites him; Salzman refuses to introduce his daughter Stella to Leo; Leo pictures in Stella "his own redemption"; and Salzman chants for the dead.

2. a. Leo, having been persuaded that "he might find it easier to win himself a congregation if he were married," seeks a marriage of convenience.

   b. After the Lily Hirschorn incident, Leo rejects this idea and the traditions of his upbringing and shifts his quest toward sexual, romantic love.

3. a. Lily poses many questions that force Leo into an inward search that gives him new knowledge about himself. For one thing Leo discovers that he "came to God not because [as he says] I loved Him, but because I did not."

   b. Inevitably, Leo sees himself as a person "unloved and loveless" and someone who did not love God or humanity as well as he might.

4. Leo dismisses Salzman because the matchmaker has failed to provide a suitable bride; Leo cannot find Salzman when he is needed most; and Salzman refuses to introduce Leo to Stella, whom Salzman describes as a wild one, one without shame, who "should burn in hell."

5. a. In the final scene when Leo goes to meet Stella, he achieves his goal.

   b. He achieves "his own redemption."

6. In finding love and resolving to "convert her [Stella] to goodness," Leo has discovered his true purpose and his relationship to God and humanity.

7. Stella can be seen as both sinful (her pose against the lamppost, the smoking, the red color as reminders of her past transgressions) and innocent (the white color, her eyes filled with desperate innocence), as if she too sought redemption. "The violins and lit candles revolved in the sky" as if the Heavens approved of this union (communion), which results in regeneration for both Leo and Stella. Salzman "chanted prayers for the dead," which may be taken figuratively to mean the death of Leo's earlier misdirected commitment, Stella's promiscuity, and Salzman's deceitful nature.

Edith Wharton

ROMAN FEVER

1. Mrs. Slade: overassertive, unscrupulous, articulate, self-assured, hard, insensitive, worldly, revengeful, envious, unfulfilled, and socially successful.

   Mrs. Ansley: conventional, once beautiful, wishy-washy, drab, quiet, sweet, gentle, sentimental, fulfilled, and a social failure.

2. a. Mrs. Slade forces the important action by bringing up incidents from the past.

   b. Mrs. Ansley is Mrs. Slade's antagonist.

   c. Mrs. Slade's final attempt at revenge backfires, and Mrs. Ansley emerges the victor, crushing Mrs. Slade's feelings of superiority.

3. a. Mrs. Slade questions how Horace and Mrs. Ansley ever produced such a brilliant child as Barbara; she refers to her daughter as an angel (vs. Barbara's brilliance); she refers to Mrs. Ansley's great-aunt as "dreadfully wicked"; and she accuses her friend of having tried to steal from her the man to whom she was engaged.

b. Mrs. Slade feels superior to Mrs. Ansley; she hates her and yet fears Mrs. Ansley's sweetness.

4. Mrs. Ansley is a quiet, sweet, gentle, honest person constantly being hurt by the hard, insensitive, revengeful Mrs. Slade.

5. Great-aunt Harriet helps the reader believe in Mrs. Ansley's having Barbara.

6. a. "Roman Fever" has little action and little emotional intensity.

   b. Critics generally consider the story remarkable because of the ingenuity of its tightly knit plot.

7. a. The last sentence serves as the resolution.

   b. Mrs. Ansley deals the final blow and "moves ahead" of Mrs. Slade in every respect.

8. Possible interpretations: Quality or superiority is guaranteed not by wealth or material possessions but only by the innate good qualities of a person; a superior mother will generally produce a superior child; a psychologically cruel person gains personal satisfaction by putting down others; cruelty will find its own punishment.

Guy deMaupassant

THE NECKLACE

1. Mme. Loisel, "born in a family of clerks," has "no dresses, no jewels, nothing," and she wants "nothing but that." With great difficulty M. Loisel obtains a special invitation for his wife to attend a minister's ball where the "whole official world" will be present. Unselfishly, M. Loisel gives his wife four hundred francs with which she can purchase a gown and suggests that she borrow some jewels from a friend. At the ball Mme. Loisel is a great success. Prettily dressed and bejeweled, she is "elegant, gracious, smiling, and crazy with joy," until she discovers the loss of the necklace. Unable to find the ornament, Mme. Loisel tells Mme. Forestier a lie. Forced to borrow a large sum of money, the Loisels buy a replacement, an expensive necklace, which they return to Mme. Forestier. For ten long years they suffer deprivation in order to pay their debt. But, at long last, Mme. Loisel is able to face Mme. Forestier, admit to the loss of the necklace, confess her lie, and reveal her poverty, only to learn that the lost necklace had no real value. However, as a consequence of her experience, Mme. Loisel's false values have been replaced by genuine values; she has gained inner peace; and her marriage seems to be happier.

2. The middle-class values are beauty, youth, social status, and material possessions.

3. As obsessed as she is with acquiring possessions that will give her status among the rich, she naturally chooses the necklace among several pieces of jewelry. Later, at the ball, ashamed of the modest wrap she is wearing over her gown, she rapidly descends the stairs to the street in order to avoid unpleasant remarks from the other women, who are dressed in furs. Her attention is so fixed on the opinion others will have of her that she scarcely notices what she is doing.

4. Having been educated in a nineteenth-century convent, where education was available to young women from all walks of life, and as lovely and charming a person as she was, Mme. Loisel was destined to make a friend or two.

5. M. Loisel loves his wife, understands her suffering, and does all he can to alleviate her pain. He goes to a great deal of trouble to get her an invitation, gives her four hundred francs, suggests a lie to buy time, retraces their steps on foot in search of the lost necklace, borrows money from usurers and lenders, and takes on an extra evening job to pay their exorbitant debt.

6. They are faced with an impossible debt which will take over ten years to pay, and they might be discovered in a lie.

7. At first Mme. Loisel is motivated by middle-class pride and false values. She is vain, obsessed with social position and material gain, immersed in self-pity, and unhappily married. Toward the end, she has apparently gained a measure of wisdom and inner peace. Her values have changed, her marriage improved, and her life is more worthwhile.

8. Protagonist: Mme. Loisel
Prize: to have the delicacies and luxuries of life
Obstacle: her pride and poverty
Point of Attack: invitation to the minister's ball
Complications: she has no appropriate dress and no jewelry
Climax: the loss of the necklace
Resolution: replacement of the necklace
Theme: Material possession is not the substance of genuine
values and does not insure happiness.

9. At the conclusion of the story, Mme. Loisel no longer "suffers ceaselessly," for she "smiles with a joy which was proud and naive at once."

10. If we accept the theme that material values do not bring happiness, the last sentence does not alter the meaning of the story. What the surprise ending does is emphasize the point that one must pay the price for falseness.

CHAPTER 2   CHARACTER

John Steinbeck

THE CHRYSANTHEMUMS

1. a. Steinbeck's early description of Elisa conveys the idea of
      suppressed femininity; her masculine garb conceals her wo-
      manly potential.

   b. The environment heightens Elisa's conflict and intensifies
      her sense of claustrophobia. Salinas Valley, a man's world,
      has forced Elisa to assume a masculinity that disallows her
      natural womanly self.

2. Steinbeck describes Elisa as a woman of great energy, "over-
   eager, over-powerful," when she cuts down the old chrysanthemum
   stalks. The ability she has to grow things suggests her crea-
   tivity, and the loving care she gives her beautiful flowers may
   serve as compensation for the children she never had. Another
   incident, the one with the tinker, makes Elisa feel like a woman
   again. Her womanliness aroused, she removes her masculine hat
   and gloves and reaches out "toward his legs" only to be denied.
   The scene illustrates Elisa's hunger for fulfillment of her emotional and physical needs.

3. Elisa tears off her masculine identity, thoroughly scrubs herself clean, scrutinizes her body in a mirror, dresses slowly
   in the "newest and nicest" feminine undergarments and dress, and
   carefully puts on her make-up. She is beautiful and as feminine
   as she has been in a long time; perhaps now she feels certain
   that she will attract her husband.

4. a. Elisa's conflict is twofold. The internal struggle is be-
      tween Elisa's desire to fulfill herself as a woman and her
      desire to yield to the life to which she has become accus-
      tomed; the external struggle involves the failure of Henry
      and the peddler to realize and grasp the potential within
      her.

   b. "Crying weakly--like an old woman," Elisa accepts her old way
      of life with some regret.

5. The tinker exposes facets of Elisa's character and reveals the
   conflict.

7

6. Yes. Elisa has camoflaged her femininity with masculine clothes, sublimated her feelings with garden work, and reached for fulfillment toward both the tinker and her husband. After being rebuffed and humiliated, we find her "crying weakly--like an old woman," realizing perhaps that her womanhood is not merely suppressed, but irrevocably lost. Thus, she admits defeat and resigns herself to her customary way of life.

7. a. Henry is sketched simply with few surface details; consequently, we know little about him.

   b. He is a flat, static character.

   c. His chief function is to reveal some aspects of Elisa's character and give credence to her motivations.

8. a. The peddler appeals to Elisa's womanliness and makes explicit her quest for sexual identity.

   b. Her actions serve as a substitute for the emotional experience she seeks.

   c. Elisa possesses an inner strength of mind that prevents her from being more aggressive toward the peddler. In a sense she then resists further temptation. The reader may also take the statement ironically because Elisa's strength appears to be superficial as she breaks down at the conclusion of the story.

William Faulkner

A ROSE FOR EMILY

1. In a society that is constantly changing, Miss Emily struggles to maintain the values of the aristocratic Old South that the Grierson family represents. Year by year Miss Emily loses contact with reality, and in the end she becomes insane.

2. The narrator describes Miss Emily as "dear, inescapable, impervious, tranquil, and perverse." The townspeople view her as "a tradition, a duty, and a care." Controlled by the values of an old aristocratic tradition, especially family pride and honor, Miss Emily lives in the past with dust and shadows. Unable to face reality, she distorts it. She claims she has no taxes to pay; she refuses to admit that her father is dead; and she determines to have a fiancé--alive or dead.

3. a. Once a symbolic shrine to former grandeur, the Grierson house is now "left, lifting its stubborn and coquettish decay above the cotton wagons and the gasoline pumps--an eyesore among eyesores." The interior is sunless. The stairway "smelled of dust and disuse--a close, dank smell." The furniture is heavy, leather-covered, and cracked. And on a

8

tarnished gilt easel before the fireplace stands a crayon portrait of Miss Emily's dead father.

b. The physical and the historical setting, rooted in the old Southern aristocratic tradition, which the Sartoris and Grierson families represent, exerted considerable influence on Miss Emily. But now she, like the house, stands proud yet decadent—a fallen monument.

4. The Sartoris and Grierson families ranked family pride and honor above all other human values. Colonel Sartoris put the family name above the economic needs and concerns of Jefferson when he concocted a story that relieved Miss Emily of having to pay taxes. Miss Emily's father held the Grierson pride in such esteem that he thought no young man good enough for his daughter. These values have shaped the character of Miss Emily.

5. Miss Emily acts according to the dictates of her own established nature. She asserts the Grierson pride with everyone she meets. When Homer Barron attempts to jilt Miss Emily, it is in character for her, who has been denied the love of a man, to murder her lover in order to keep him, even in death.

6. The reluctance of the Old South's aristocracy to change furnishes a clue to meaning. Miss Emily, who symbolizes this tradition, exerts her will and superiority over anyone who chooses to oppose her. She is therefore able to retain her values until she loses contact with reality and dies.

7. The story embodies a complex set of attitudes toward the declining Southern aristocratic tradition. Faulkner offers this psychological truth: no one can really escape reality. Through the years attitudes change and we must change with them or suffer the consequences.

8. Homer's chief function is to furnish a contrast to the character of Miss Emily. She is a Southerner, aristocratic, steeped in family tradition, which suggests permanency, friendlessness, and a lady of breeding. Homer is a Northerner, a laborer with no known tradition, a transient, friendly with everyone, and a man who shows his coarseness by using foul language, drinking, and smoking.

9. In the title, a rose is given to Emily. Faulkner, through his narrator, perhaps tries to give Emily a token of his love for the love she never really had. Further, he may wish to honor the memory of her struggle to maintain her traditional values.

Flannery O'Connor

EVERYTHING THAT RISES MUST CONVERGE

1. Julian's mother was reared on a Southern plantation that had two
   hundred slaves. It was a period of strict moral standards and
   of narrow vision toward change. She therefore speaks and acts
   for the older generation and maintains the old values and attitudes.

2. Julian's mother sees herself as one who believes in the code of
   Southern gentility. She obviously considers those values superior to Julian's values because she adheres to the status quo and
   fails to see that the days of old have passed. Julian sees his
   mother as an old fool--ignorant, hypocritical, and dishonest,
   blindly holding onto a system of values inferior to his.

3. Julian perceives himself as a member of the new generation--in-
   telligent, tolerant, honest, and understanding--whose system of
   values is superior to his mother's. We are disgusted with Julian over his cruel and insensitive treatment of his mother; we
   pity him for his own prejudices and his failure to face reality;
   and we may even sympathize with him when, at the end of the
   story, we come to realize that without his mother, Julian will
   be lost completely.

4. Julian's mother behaves childishly when she repeats several
   sayings, all of which are clichés, for example, "Rome wasn't
   built in a day"; when she vacillates about whether or not to
   purchase the hat; and when she reacts to an unpleasantness from
   Julian by saying, "I'll just go home."

5. Any significant change in setting would alter the effects of
   this particular story as written. The experience from which the
   story is told is uniquely Southern.

6. For Julian's mother the hat is an emblem of the social and personal values she holds; for Julian it is her "ridiculous ban-
   ner," showing off her prejudices. The identical hat worn by the
   black woman suggests equality.

7. The story deals with black/white relations. The conflict is
   introduced when Julian's mother purchases a hat which to her
   implies superiority. Shortly afterward, a black woman enters
   the bus with her little boy; she wears an identical hat. Julian is pleased and hopes the incident will teach his mother a
   lesson--i.e., he hopes the meeting will help him to re-emphasize
   a point to his mother about the error of her views. However,
   "the lesson had rolled off her like rain on a roof." In a
   show of kindness, Julian's mother offers the little boy a
   penny, which infuriates the woman. With her pocketbook, she as-
   saults Julian's mother, who falls to the ground. Not only does
   Julian's mother suffer embarrassment, but she also suffers a
   stroke. Only when Julian realizes the seriousness of her af-
   fliction does he desperately cry for her.

8. Presumably, Julian's mother suffers a stroke. The mention of her high blood pressure in the opening sentence gives credibility to this sudden attack.

9. At the end, we discover that there is now no solid ground under Julian--the source of his strength is gone.

W. Somerset Maugham

THE COLONEL'S LADY

1. George Peregrine is an egotist. His self-centeredness and superficiality so distort his attitude and point of view that he cannot understand anyone or anything. His point of view is subjective and never objective. His interests and concerns are consequently narrow and inevitably focused on himself.

2. Both are popular among the people of the village. Evie is a genuinely fine person, and George is a public-spirited person who does good deeds apparently to be known as a "jolly good fellow."

3. George's major flaw is egotism. Examples abound: He is glad Evie used her maiden name on the title page of the book; he would appreciate her not talking about him to her friends; strolling by two women who are sitting together on a sofa, he has the impression that they are talking about him; and the love story in the poem makes him out a "damned fool, a laughing stock." "She wouldn't have written that book unless she hated me," George says.

4. Everyone adores Evie except George. He blames her for having no heir; he procures for himself a mistress on the pretext that "a man, a healthy normal man had to have some fun in his life"; and he doesn't suppose her work will ever amount to anything-- "damned silly title" and "long lines of irregular length and didn't rhyme"--when literary critics praise her work. Finally, supposing that the love affair alluded to in Evie's book must have been a true experience, George informs his attorney that he cannot go on living with a woman who has been "grossly unfaithful." The reader knows that George's view of Edie is unfair and thus sympathizes with her.

5. Society looks at George through rose-colored glasses. It views him as a kind, benevolent, respectable gentleman in the community.

6. Maugham presents the truth about George and sharply brings it into focus when Henry Blane, the attorney, tells George that his ego gets in the way of everything and that it is morally wrong for him to put his pride above all else. Just as George is myopic, so is society.

7. George is a static character. The conflict through which he passes teaches him nothing. He does not change. Refer to the last sentence in the story.

8. Maugham's intrusion in the action of the story provides the reader with the author's attitude toward his characters. Consider, for example, the scene in which George meets the critic Dashwood.

9. If we are to judge others, we must judge them by the same standards by which we ourselves are willing to be judged.

Carson McCullers

A TREE, A ROCK, A CLOUD

1. a. The narrator is perfectly suited to tell the story, standing nearly invisible, outside the action, remaining neutral, and reporting the events objectively.

   b. None of the characters could tell the story as effectively as the narrator. The transient is too close to the experience of love to be reliable; Leo is depicted as bitter and loveless; and the young paper boy knows little or nothing about the subject of love.

2. a. The transient tries to enlighten the boy about the nature of love. The man delivers his sermon to protect the boy from making the same mistakes he has made.

   b. The transient fails to make a believer out of the boy.

   c. The boy is too immature to comprehend the significance of the communication.

3. a. The "mean, stingy, and loveless" Leo functions as a contrast to the transient and his concept of love, and to the boy, whose naiveté about such matters apparently remains unchanged.

   b. The boy turns to Leo, an older, supposedly wiser and more experienced man than he, for agreement. "Was he crazy? Do you think he was a lunatic?...Leo? Or not?"

   c. Perhaps Leo feels that his answer might further confuse the boy.

4. a. Only Leo seems to be affected by the transient's message.

   b. Leo changes from an attitude of bitterness to one of meditative silence.

5. The setting helps us to understand the story's meaning by representing a bright place where people can escape from the dark.

The contrasts suggest the differences between the inhospitable nature of the outside world, where the transient's science of love is not yet known, and the friendly atmosphere of the café, where the illumination is to take place.

6. The theme proposes the need to love "scientifically"--that is, to love first simple things and then graduate to the more complex nature of another person. The title alludes to this message about love.

7. Protagonist: the transient
   Prize: to enlighten the boy
   Obstacle: the boy's immaturity
   Point of Attack: the transient says, "I love you...."
   Complications: Leo's concept of love; his insults and loss of temper
   Climax: Leo screams for the transient to shut up
   Resolution: the boy fails to get the message
   Theme: A person cannot be enlightened without the capacity or readiness to be enlightened.

Sherwood Anderson

I WANT TO KNOW WHY

1. a. The narrator is thoughtful, sensitive, and youthfully idealistic.

   b. Generally he can be counted on to be reliable in the actions he takes and the important statements he makes. His love for horses and the natural beauty of the surroundings; his feelings toward his father, Bildad, Tillford, the bad woman, and others; his questioning of the various accepted values of the adult world; and his discoveries and disillusionments are indeed genuine and believable.

   c. Being the youthful romantic that he is, the boy is sometimes unreliable. He cannot help but color a few of his well-intentioned remarks with a veneer of prejudice or make such sweeping generalizations as the following: "White men will do that [squeal on kids], but not a nigger."

2. The author devotes most of the story to a meticulous portrayal of the character of the boy. The actual incident that the narrator wants to report occupies only the last fifth of the story.

3. a. The boy is a dynamic character. The discovery of how evil touches adults whom he especially loves shocks him. Although the experience may be necessary in the process of growing up, the realization strikes a blow to his youthful idealism.

b. The dilemma involves the boy's struggle to maintain his ideals in the face of reality, which displays an adult world contaminated with false values.

c. He is a boy who idealizes horses and appreciates natural beauty in the world; he wants "to think straight and be O.K." Consequently, when the boy discovers evil in the people he admires, he is shocked, hurt, and disillusioned.

4. Loving horses as he does, the boy "beats his way on freight cars" to Sarasota for the racing season. He admires Bildad, who works with horses, because he is square with kids. He would like to be like Bildad: to "think straight and be O.K." He idolizes Tillford, who trains Sunstreak, his favorite of the two great horses. But when he sees Tillford drunk, taking credit for Sunstreak's world-record race and kissing the "tall rotten-looking woman" at the farmhouse, the boy loses his youthful, idealistic world. The setting, the characters, and the incidents all unite and contribute to a structural unity that focuses on the theme.

5. The title and the statement "I want to know why" hint at the theme and re-echo a protest against the evil the boy finds in the adult world of false values.

6. The boy wants to know why Jerry Tillford, his friend who also loves horses, loves prostitutes. Why Tillford does not "think straight and be O.K." Why evil. Why ugliness, prejudices, and false values. His questions add up to why life must be as it is and not as good and beautiful as it was before the experience at the farmhouse.

7. All the qualities the boy admires in horses are, he feels, qualities people should possess.

8. a. To the boy, anyone associated with horses is good. Bildad automatically deserves admiration because he likes horses and lives "where horses are and where men like to come and talk about horses." Furthermore, Bildad possesses many good qualities: he always does little favors for people; he can flatter anyone into letting him do anything he wants; he can keep a secret; and he can cook a good meal.

b. Bildad helps to illustrate the theme. When the boy says about Bildad, "I wish I was a nigger," and again, "I would like to be a stable boy, but had to give that up too. Mostly niggers do that work and I knew father wouldn't let me go into it. No use to ask him," the boy is growing up, recognizing people for what they are and not for what society says they are.

FICTION

D. H. Lawrence

THE HORSE DEALER'S DAUGHTER

1. Lawrence introduces a problem which will require an important decision by Mabel, and he establishes a desolate and dreamy mood.

2. At the beginning Lawrence is objective; then he shifts into Mabel's consciousness and later enters Dr. Fergusson's mind.

3. Mabel, whose security is threatened by the collapse of her family, lives an incomparably futile existence. The despair that envelops Mabel leads to her mother's tomb, where she feels momentarily secure, and later to the foul, winter pond, where she attempts suicide by drowning. Fergusson, whose life is characterized by a similar deadness, enters the pond (although not a swimmer) and rescues her. Both rise out of murky water rejuvenated.

4. a. The opening portions of the story, which introduce the setting and the mood of frustration, are presented objectively. The narrative here is simple and straightforward.

   b. After the kiss, we enter the consciousness of Dr. Fergusson to share his inner feelings and doubts of the moment.

   c. Lawrence employs the dramatic mode of presentation for the first third of his story until he shifts point of view to Mabel's consciousness. The scene in which the brothers advise Mabel to go live with Lucy is heightened dramatically by the use of dialogue.

   d. The exposition about Joseph Pervin, which immediately follows this scene, presents a good example of the summary method. It furnishes many years of background information, from the time the family enjoyed wealth to their present status.

5. a. Both Mabel and Dr. Fergusson can serve as protagonists.

   b. The experience changes both characters.

   c. Mabel better fits our definition of a protagonist.

   d. The story focuses more sharply on Mabel, her family, her past, her problem, and her motivation.

6. a. Dr. Fergusson frets continually about himself. He performs his duties perfunctorily, without physical or spiritual stimulation.

   b. His chief motivation appears to be a sensitivity to Mabel's conflict.

   c. We may or may not accept it as sufficient preparation for
      Dr. Fergusson's risking his life to save Mabel and his fal-
      ling in love with her.

7. Dr. Fergusson's loss of his only friend, his passionless attitude toward his patients and his work, and his recognition of
   Mabel's "heavy power" furnish adequate preparation for his falling in love.

8. The final love scene casts light on Dr. Fergusson's motives,
   points to Mabel as a symbol of the "death wish" and to Dr.
   Fergusson as a symbol of the "life wish," defines a particular
   kind of love, and reveals the theme.

F. Scott Fitzgerald

BABYLON REVISITED

1. Protagonist: Charlie Wales
   Prize: custody of his daughter
   Obstacle: his inability to escape the past
   Point of Attack: his announcement that he is in Paris to see
     his little girl
   Complications: his visits to old haunts, Marion Peters's re-
     sentfulness of Charlie, his meeting of old friends Lorraine
     and Duncan, Charlie's lack of confidence in himself, Marion's
     blaming Charlie for Helen's death
   Climax: Lorraine and Duncan's surprise visit at the Peters's
     house, which upsets Marion
   Resolution: Marion postpones the decision about Honoria for
     six months
   Theme: One cannot escape the past and the responsibility for
     one's sins.

2. Charlie is handsome and rich, having amassed his wealth chiefly
   through hard work after losing a fortune during the stock mar-
   ket crash of 1929. His period of dissipation consisted of
   drunken sprees and some meaningless, irresponsible episodes.
   By sheer willpower he conquers his alcoholism, avoids temptation from the past, and keeps his temper under wraps. But the
   ever-present past affects Charlie like a nightmare, and his
   lack of confidence in himself destroys his hopes for the future.

3. a. Marion Peters is a neurotic woman who lives in a little world
     which is not as secure as she believes. Most of her actions
     and reactions are irrational and unreasonable. Jealous of
     Charlie for the wild life he has had and the wealth he has
     accumulated, she shows her bitter resentment by making ugly
     references to the past and condemning Charlie for the death
     of Helen.

   b. Lorraine Quarrles and Duncan Schaeffer are antagonists to
     Charlie. They are what he once was--careless, frivolous,
     fun-loving, irresponsible. They are part of his inecapable

past. Their presence and intrusion destroy what hope Charlie might have had for the future.

4. All of the characters are ghosts of the past. They furnish information about Charlie which serves as a painful reminder of what he might have become if he had not mastered his alcoholism. Lincoln Peters has a larger role: he seems to understand Charlie and sympathize with him. He is the sensible, reasonable, rational mediator between Charlie and Marion.

5. a. After a whirlwind life of partying with companions everywhere he went, a wife and daughter nearby, Charlie finds himself alone because he has changed his life. He begins to realize, though too late, that the people that really matter are his wife and daughter, both of whom he has lost.

   b. The scenery in Paris has changed and, of course, so has Charlie, who now sees things through a realistic perspective. The scenery reminds him constantly of what he was, what he might have become, and what he has lost.

6. Part II furnishes background information, advances the story, reveals character, and foreshadows further intervention from the ghosts of the past.

7. a. Honoria suggests honor; Wales suggests the homonym <u>wails</u>, as well as alluding to nobility; and Quarrles implies the quarrels Lorraine has caused among Charlie, his wife, and Marion.

   b. These names and places are well-known to upper-middle-class American expatriates who lived in Paris between World War I and World War II, and make the story seem more real.

   c. Charlie Wales views the Paris he loved during the late twenties as a Babylon--the ancient city that symbolizes corruption and moral decadence. The characters' utter irresponsibility contributes to a period of dissipation.

8. He conveys value judgments about these people, since the colors carry connotations about their characters.

9. a. The story is told from the third-person point of view.

   b. Voice: Third person
      Consciousness: We have access to the narrator's consciousness
      Position and Presence: The story is told through the eyes of an outside observer
      Reliability: The narrator is reliable. A reasonable objectivity is achieved despite the fact that the narrator shares Charlie's feelings and toward the end of the story the two are nearly inseparable.
      In addition, this point of view provides a marked sense of realism, gives the story a semblance of unity, permits the

author to intrude via the narrator, and establishes an inti-
mate relationship between the characters and the reader.

CHAPTER 4   THEME OR MEANING

Stephen Crane

THE OPEN BOAT

1. Each part of "The Open Boat" contributes to some extent to the
   advancement of the story and to the development of character,
   but the primary focus of each part is on theme.

2. a. The four men serve as a composite protagonist.

   b. The conflict is the men's struggle against the irrational,
      lawless, and uncontrollable forces of nature.

3. The oiler, the hardiest of the group, who exerts the greatest
   physical effort to save himself and the other members of the
   crew, drowns solely by chance. His death, grimly ironic, shows
   the indifference of nature or the arbitrariness of fate.

4. a. The correspondent's early attitude toward the Algerian sol-
      dier is one of indifference.

   b. His new feeling of compassion derives from the realization
      that only when individuals become aware of their true posi-
      tion and purpose in life can they pity and love their bro-
      thers (humanity).

5. a. The naked rescuer illustrates another aspect of the theme of
      brotherhood, suggesting that people can seek solace (in this
      case rescue) only from those who share a common bond of love
      and understanding.

   b. The men now feel that they can understand nature, their po-
      sition and relationship to it.

   c. The remark points to a new awareness in the correspondent, a
      change in attitude from unconcern to compassion for humanity.

6. a. "They see nature first as malevolently hostile and then as
      thoughtlessly hostile": see Mordecai Marcus, "The Three-
      fold View of Nature in 'The Open Boat,'" Philological
      Quarterly XLI (April 1962), 511-515, for an excellent arti-
      cle on the naturalistic view of nature.

b. Finally, they see nature as serene but totally indifferent.

7. a. The drowning of the oiler and the survival of the sailors suggest nature's indifference and arbitrariness.

   b. Nature does not regard human beings as important; fate controls the lives of all human beings; suffering makes men brothers.

8. The final sentence implies that the experience the men have had gives them new insight into the character of nature. They finally believe nature to be indifferent.

9. Students might give a variety of answers that explore the universal truth that "tragedy makes men brothers."

James Joyce

ARABY

1. "Araby" is a story of disillusionment. A boy, reared in a dead, empty neighborhood for a moment journeys to a rich, promising place, only to find there a cold, dark world; his dream is shattered. The story begins with a physical emptiness and ends with an intellectual emptiness.

2. The first two paragraphs establish the setting of the story, which prepares the reader for its thematic emphasis.

3. The boy's neighborhood is described as sterile, empty, and dead. The house has been abandoned; it is located on a dead-end street; the priest has died; the bicycle pump is rusty and unusable; the papers are useless and the books are decaying; and the few bushes are dying.

4. The scene at the bazaar is the occasion of the boy's final disillusionment. He discovers that there is no hope there, only the final defeat of his dream.

5. a. The boy expected to find love, enchantment, and fulfillment.

   b. Instead, he finds inane conversation, deception, and materialism, which completely disillusions him.

6. Significant episodes include the boy's visit to the priest's house, his meeting of Mangan's sister, the solitary journey to Araby, and the experience at the bazaar.

7. The young boy would have lacked the wisdom and experience to evaluate what happened, while a mature person can discover the significance of childhood events.

8. The religious symbols and references include the wild garden
   (the Garden of Eden), the central apple tree (the Tree of
   Life), the Christian Brothers' School, "shrill litanies," "nas-
   al chanting," "strange prayers," and the bearing of the chalice. They contribute to our understanding of the story's religious theme: the boy's quest for relevance in modern religion ends in failure.

9. a. The major theme that the story suggests is that the church
      and contemporary religion hold little meaning for people
      today.

   b. Araby represents the church, which came out of the East.
      Much of the description of the bazaar--like a cathedral,
      the silence, and the big hall--fits this idea.

   c. The title complements the religious symbols and imagery to
      suggest a religious theme.

10. The young boy sees darkness instead of light. He feels ridi-
    culed by the futility of his efforts in search of meaning. In-
    stead of fulfillment he finds hollowness and worthlessness.
    His eyes burn with pain and anger at what he sees.

Shirley Jackson

THE LOTTERY

1. a. All the townspeople serve as the protagonist.

   b. They are typical of every man and every woman and represent
      the two sides of humanity--"decency" on the one hand, "sav-
      agery" on the other--upon which the story develops.

   c. The literal prize is escape from death, and the ironic prize
      is death itself.

2. The author views blind acceptance of tradition, ritual, and old
   values as a danger to society. The conflict in this story occurs within each character and must be inferred: the pull of
   tradition fights the human capacity to make moral judgments.
   The pull of tradition wins and this victory points to a variety
   of thematic interpretations.

3. a. By perpetuating old customs and tradition without re-examin-
      ing their real meaning, people tend to act cruelly toward
      one another. The author also shows the dichotomy in human
      nature by showing decent, friendly folks who practice mean-
      ingless customs that result in senseless cruelty to others.

   b. The townspeople are friendly and mean well but accept with-
      out question the old ways and continue these practices as
      always. The lottery is an annual affair enjoyed by everyone;

all citizens of the community must be present; the rules are presented and clarified each year; they must be observed, and so on. No one questions the lottery, its purpose, its method, its meaning. Only Mrs. Hutchinson, after learning that she is the one to be sacrificed, protests that the whole thing is unfair. As is the custom, all villagers pick up their stones and pitch them at the victim.

4. a. All are social types: Old Man Warner represents the bigoted reactionary; Mr. Summers is the prototype of civic duty; Mr. and Mrs. Adams are the liberals; Mrs. Hutchinson is the egotist; and Mrs. Delacroix is the two-faced person, friendly to Mrs. Hutchinson before the lottery and vicious to her afterward.

   b. All of the characters together make up the complex nature of humanity.

5. The author achieves suspense by withholding information from the reader. All we know at first is that something extraordinary is going on. There is a drawing, but we do not know what for. There will be a winner, but who the winner will be or what he or she will win remains a mystery until the final scene.

6. Before Tessie is a victim, she accepts the old ritual and the lottery with noticeable unconcern. She had nearly forgotten what day this was. But once she is chosen, she naturally protests loudly about the unfairness of the lottery.

7. By developing one character more fully and presenting the story through that person's consciousness, the author might have gained more sympathy for the victim. But a more informed central character might have given away the grim surprise ending. Furthermore, the eerie mood and atmosphere might have lost effectiveness.

8. The author's ample use of realistic details throughout the story and the controlled objectivity with which the story develops make this unbelievable story believable.

9. This requires a personal response.

Robert Fontaine

SIX BEAUTIES

1. The story begins with Uncle Desmonde's announcement of his imminent death, the consequence of high blood pressure, presumably caused by an irreverent passion for rich foods and good wines. After a fainting spell, a doctor is summoned and he prescribes a strict diet, which Desmonde is quick to ignore. Naturally, the pressure rises and the concerned family calls a conference to determine the proper course of action. It is at this point

that we learn about Desmonde's unusual parting wishes. In addition to a rich menu, he requests the presence of six of Canada's most beautiful women. His out-of-the-ordinary request is that they wear a large hat, long black gloves, black stockings, and nothing else. Father Sebastian is called in and told of Uncle Desmonde's farewell banquet. The family merely seeks the priest's opinion about the pageant: "Is it bad? Or is it good?" After much thought, the priest declares, "It will depend...on the choice of wines."

2. Uncle Desmonde is a strong-willed, amusing eccentric. He is a bon vivant with a passion for rich foods, good wine, and beautiful women.

3. Uncle Desmonde presumably wins, since Father Sebastian approves of his plan.

4. Maman's function is to bring common sense and understanding to the character of Uncle Desmonde. Felix appears to serve as the antagonist who seriously questions Uncle Desmonde's plans.

5. Fontaine achieves suspense by presenting important information gradually, as needed for effect. We are given details about Uncle Desmonde's specific plans not at once, but over a period of time.

6. The main theme is that life should be a joy to the very end. It is revealed chiefly through the characters, their joie de vivre, their witty form of speech, and, of course, through Uncle Desmonde's plan.

7. "Six Beauties" is an amusing story. The entertainment derives from the originality of the plot and characters and the clever dialogue.

Ernest Hemingway

HILLS LIKE WHITE ELEPHANTS

1. Hemingway's near-total dependence on dialogue moves the story
   quickly forward and achieves dramatic objectivity. The style
   may be bothersome, however, and since we know little about the
   characters, we lose a certain amount of sympathy for them, and
   perhaps we fail to see meaning.

2. Dialogue is used extensively. It is typical of Hemingway:
   clear, terse, cogent, vivid, and believable.

3. The man does not care for the baby or respect the young woman's wishes. Theirs is a useless, empty, sterile kind of existence.

4. He is rejecting responsibility, change, the opportunity for
   growth and fulfillment; instead, he is embracing the status
   quo--the pointlessness of their lives.

5. The man and the young woman are not compatible. The man's
   literal response and irritable manner when the young woman
   reveals a sensitive nature in her observation that the hills
   across the river look like white elephants suggest incompati-
   bility.

6. The station serves to emphasize the couple's transient, imper-
   manent, homeless, directionless lives.

7. Examples of understatement:

   a. The young woman quietly delivers a pronouncement of desper-
      ation when she says, "And we could have all this...."

   b. The couple's quarrel begins so quietly that the reader is
      slow to realize that the two are indeed arguing.

   c. After all possibilities for reconciliation have been ex-
      hausted, the young woman quietly threatens, "I'll scream."

Hemingway uses understatement chiefly for shock effect. The technique also serves to heighten the couple's hostility.

8. Professor Lionel Trilling (Columbia University) suggests the following: when the girl looks at the line of hills in one direction and sees "the country brown and dry," she sees the landscape of sterility. On the other hand, when she stands up and walks to the end of the station and sees "fields of grain and trees along the banks of the Ebro," she sees the landscape of peace of fecundity. These two scenes represent symbolically the two choices available to the girl.

9. Thematically, the story focuses on a sterile, empty, monotonous, pointless, desperate way of life and points to a lost opportunity for growth, fulfillment, and happiness.

10. Hemingway has disassociated himself from the reader and the characters in the story. He tells us very little about the young woman and the man, their background, appearance, names (except for the girl's nickname, Jig), ages, gestures, tone of voice, or marital status. The tone is impersonal; explanations are rare, as are author intrusions; the resolution is unclear, and the meaning is vague.

Ralph Ellison

KING OF THE BINGO GAME

1. a. Ellison's purpose is to show the injustices perpetrated against blacks in American society.

   b. The broad issue addressed is the condition of and the place held by blacks in American democracy.

   c. The design the author employs to get his meaning across is effective.

   d. To achieve his special effects, Ellison makes use of several narrative devices which take him beyond realism without losing plausibility. These techniques include the omission of the protagonist's name, the symbolic bingo wheel and trial, the setting in a theater, and the severely limited point of view.

2. a. Ellison suggests that a person from the minority group (in this case, a young black man) is generally a loser in the midst of the majority (here, white society). He feels helpless because he has no way of changing this general condition.

   b. Such persons have no real identity.

3. The bingo wheel represents the wheel of life controlled by chance. Only when the young man has his fingers on "the button of power and control" does he know who he is, and only then does he feel he can guide his own destiny. Ellison gives many clues to this meaning, such as "He felt vaguely that his whole life was determined by the bingo wheel."

4. The reader is made to experience precisely what the young man feels, running out of breath along with him.

5. The crowd at the theater lacks understanding; it is unruly, mocking, and even cruel. Its behavior dramatically emphasizes the plight of the black people.

6. a. The young player feels that his entire life (past, present, and future), is in the hands of others. He is powerless.

   b. He questions the crowd's lack of understanding. There is a power within him that compels him to do this and he cannot stop, for then he would lose (die).

   c. As long as he presses the button, the player is king; as long as he is in control, he has a reasonable chance of getting what he is after.

7. He comes to know himself.

8. The double zero shows that the player has lost once again; thus Ellison achieves greater sympathy for the player and his people.

9. The person in charge or in control is king. In this story we may interpret the king to mean the white population, the majority.

Eudora Welty

A WORN PATH

1. Like the mythical bird, Phoenix is old, gold-colored, and beautiful; she returns periodically to the same place to renew her life; and she has traveled a path many times that she will continue to travel, seemingly forever.

2. a. Literally, Phoenix wants to save the life of her grandson; figuratively, she wants to preserve the source of love, which gives meaning to her life and the power to persevere. Phoenix gains renewed life through her journey.

   b. The conflict involves Phoenix's encounter with the real and imaginary obstacles along the path that threaten to break a powerful spirit.

3. The hill, the thorny bushes, the log, the animals, the barbed
   wire, the scarecrow, the hunter, and the ditch are hazards
   along the path. They represent tests of faith and strength.
   Phoenix exemplifies her faith and strength through her patience,
   determination, hope, courage, skill, wisdom, firm belief in
   God, and perpetual devotion to her grandson. This love Phoenix
   transfers into good will toward all humanity. She admits no
   selfish thoughts and recognizes no class or race distinctions.

4. Lacking the qualities of love and compassion that Phoenix possesses, the people in the clinic treat her with professional
   coldness and mechanical efficiency, so she responds in kind.

5. The hunter exemplifies the imperfect nature of human beings.
   Although sufficiently concerned to help Phoenix, he is cruel.
   He kills a bird and a dog, mocks her, and lies to her.

6. The Christmas season provides the historical setting; the narrative contains several references to the colors red, green,
   and silver; during the journey Phoenix is reborn; because of
   an unhealing wound the grandson could symbolize the infant
   Jesus; and the windmill may suggest a cross, the star the
   Wise Men followed, or the gifts they brought.

7. There are numerous examples of humor in the way Phoenix speaks
   and acts. One delightful reaction occurs in the cornfield when
   she realizes that the "tall, black, and skinny" ghost is only
   a scarecrow. She laughs at herself and pretends to dance with
   the scarecrow. The humor adds a further dimension to a beautiful characterization and provides relief for a tragic situation.

8. The author achieves unity by keeping the action simple and focused on Phoenix and her journey.

9. So in tune with nature and so full of love for a grandson and
   for humanity, Phoenix can withstand any pain, make any sacrifice, and endure forever. It is this attitude toward life,
   which springs from love, that leads to the meaning of the
   story.

Kurt Vonnegut, Jr.

THE MANNED MISSILES

1. a. The conflict is between the human values of the two fathers
      and the political values of the nations they live in.

   b. The U.S. and Soviet governments are the forces warring
      against one another.

2. a. The first letter introduces the reader to the death of two
      astronauts in space. It reveals the background and charac-
      ter of the Russian family, their feelings of pride and
      grief, and their hopes for the future.

b. The second letter parallels the first letter in information about the American family and adds a few more details about what led to the death of the two young men; it contains a little more propaganda.

c. The symmetrical design of the letters allows us to see how alike people are even though they live under opposing forms of government.

3. The fathers' strong emotions appeal to a similar response from readers. A callous approach might have caused a shift in emphasis to the ideological struggles of the superpowers. With that approach the author might have lost sympathy for the innocent victims and their families and perhaps diminished the anger one feels for unjust killing.

4. a. Vonnegut achieves suspense by developing his exposition bit by bit and by withholding information. Example: in paragraph two, the young men are spoken of in the past tense. We want to ask what happened to them. At the end of paragraph four we are told that they died in space. Now we are curious about how they died.

b. Unity is achieved by the symmetrical design and content of the two letters.

5. The unwanted sacrifice of young people for the quarrels of others is sheer idiocy.

6. Vonnegut satirizes political propaganda; he exposes the folly and wickedness of two nations who strive to become the two top military powers in the world while each talks of peace.

7. The irony that the two young men have killed each other unwillingly stresses the folly of hostility between the two nations.

8. Trust one another, try to understand one another, accept the other's differences, and work cooperatively for the common good of all.

CHAPTER 6   OTHER STORIES TO READ

James Baldwin

SONNY'S BLUES

1. The revelation achieves sympathy for Mama and Sonny, and for all
   the innocent who are similarly wronged.

2. a. There may be no practical remedy that will stop trouble, but
      by being there the brother will show faith in and love for
      Sonny.

   b. Sonny disagrees with his brother, believing that if people
      cannot do what they love to do and what they want to do,
      there is no point to living.

   c. The Creole discloses what the blues are about and how his
      boys try to find new ways to make us listen. We need to be
      reminded always about our suffering, as well as our triumphs.
      This is how we learn from the past, come to understand, and
      prepare ourselves for survival.

Jorge Louis Borges

THE SHAPE OF THE SWORD

1. Surprise is achieved by withholding the unexpected truth--the
   identity of the real storyteller--until the very end.

2. From a rereading of the first paragraph we learn that the story
   was told from Moon's point of view and not from the English-
   man's. Further, we discover the true betrayer to be Moon.

3. The credibility of the story is enhanced by the revelation that
   the author is the narrator. The story is told to him, not
   through hearsay, but first-hand; we believe him because of such
   realistic observations as "I thought he was going to throw me
   out of the house" and "I noticed that his hands were shaking."

4. Yes, Moon is repentant because he reveals the secret of the
   scar and admits to his act of infamy.

OTHER STORIES TO READ

Kate Chopin

THE STORY OF AN HOUR

1. According to Mrs. Mallard, she was dominated by a husband whose intentions were both kind and cruel. Consequently, she lived a life not for herself but for him. This reveals that she regards herself as not a whole person.

2. She feels free in body and soul because now "she would live for herself."

3. The first sentence informs the reader of Mrs. Mallard's heart trouble. Answers to other possible endings and effects are subjective.

Nathaniel Hawthorne

RAPPACCINI'S DAUGHTER

1. Protagonist: Giovanni
   Prize: love of Beatrice
   Obstacle: Dr. Rappaccini's powers
   Point of Attack: Professor Baglioni's first warning to Giovanni about Dr. Rappaccini's character and wicked experiments
   Complications: two other warnings by Professor Baglioni; the withering of the test flower Giovanni buys for Beatrice; the withering of the bouquet he gives Beatrice; the spider that dies from Beatrice's breath; the meeting with Dr. Rappaccini and becoming the subject of one of the doctor's experiments; when Beatrice stops Giovanni from touching a deadly plant; when Giovanni awakes with agony in his hand
   Climax: the scene in which Giovanni accuses Beatrice of being a poisonous monster
   Resolution: Beatrice dies
   Themes: a. To be ruled totally by passion, without benefit of reason, is apt to bring disappointment, defeat, or suffering.
   b. No person has the right to violate another person's humanity.
   c. To violate the sanctity of the human heart is an unpardonable sin.

2. Hawthorne makes use of realism to establish credibility. We can readily identify with Giovanni from the opening scene. He is a young college student who is lonely because he lives in an "ill-furnished apartment" in a foreign city, away from home and family. Realistic details enhance the credibility not only of Dame Lisabetta and Professor Baglioni but even of Beatrice, who is gentle, feminine, and sweet, however peculiar her powers.

3. The type of irony that dominates the story is situation irony. It is primarily associated with the quality of beauty--the

31

beautiful Beatrice is poisonous; the magnificent garden and its lovely flowers are also poisonous. Irony here serves to underscore the theme that passion can be an evil thing.

4. Giovanni is young, handsome, healthy, bright, and honest. Beatrice is also young, beautiful, healthy, intelligent, and truthful. Both seek love; both are victimized by Dr. Rappaccini. But here the similarities cease. Giovanni, possessed by Beatrice's beauty, rejects Baglioni's warnings, disregards the young lady's strange activities, and allows his passion to rule over reason. Beatrice, gentle, unsophisticated, and full of life, is totally helpless under the control of her wicked father.

5. The imagery is consistent and appropriate to the theme. All that is beautiful--Beatrice, Giovanni, the resplendent garden, and the magnificent flowers--is not what it seems; contaminated with the poison that Dr. Rappaccini produces in his experiments, all these things are destined to perish. Although something may be "true to the outward senses, still it may be false in its essence," and so, penetrating reason, not passion, should rule.

Ann Petry

DOBY'S GONE

1. The story is told through the eyes of an outside observer. This point of view is effective as a means of promoting a strong sense of realism, enhancing the story's credibility, establishing a close relationship between Sue and the reader, and achieving a ready structural unity.

2. Doby exists only in Sue's mind, and so represents the world of make-believe. Sue treats her imaginary playmate as if he were real: Doby goes everywhere she goes, has a place next to her at the eating table, a bed next to hers, and a seat on trains and buses.

3. Once Sue stands up in a fight with her classmates and replaces her private dream world with the real world, she takes a long step toward growing up and consequently gains acceptance from her classmates.

4. Sue does not tell her mother about the fights because she has made new friends now, real ones, and to tell on them might jeopardize that relationship.

OTHER STORIES TO READ

Philip Roth

DEFENDER OF THE FAITH

1. Marx is an admirable human being, morally sensitive, compassionate, and a good soldier committed to fairness. He wants to be
   a good Jew. Grossbart's priorities differ from Marx's. He
   puts his humanity last; his Jewishness second, and himself
   first.

2. We must remember that in 1945 anti-Semitism was a prominent
   issue. The WASP looked on the Jew as a second-class citizen,
   one concerned primarily with himself and who would do anything
   for personal gain. He was supposed to be assertive, offensive,
   loud, crafty, manipulative, and dishonest. After taking care of
   himself, he looked after his own. The larger society only interested him if it served his selfish interests. Grossbart ac-
   curately portrays this stereotype.

3. Protagonist: Marx
   Conflict: he must choose between two loyalties
   Obstacle: his integrity and determination to be just

Wakako Yamauchi

THE BOATMEN ON TONEH RIVER

1. The frequent shifts of scene not only permit necessary exposition from the past to enter the story, but they keep the action
   moving at a faster pace than would otherwise be possible. In
   addition, the technique achieves suspense.

2. Kimi's mother's life has been "devoured by work, poverty, and
   anxieties"; it is reasonable to assume that Kimi's life has
   been no different from her mother's.

3. The descriptions of nature are important to our understanding
   of Kimi, who sees something "sweet and gentle" in the arid desert. Nature affords Kimi peace and solitude.

4. The father's role, similar to the mother's role, reveals the
   "soggy life-style" of their existence and their defeatist attitude toward life.

5. Protagonist: Kimi
   Prize: love
   Obstacle: the parents' inability to accept reality
   Point of Attack: Ryo's cheerfulness; refusal to accept the truth
   Complications: Mari is kept away from Kimi; the parents con-
      tinually complain; no affection is shown to Kimi
   Climax: Kimi admits her own failure and guilt
   Resolution: Kimi dies
   Theme: powerful life patterns do not change; people can affect
      changes in life patterns

Joseph Conrad

HEART OF DARKNESS

1. The narrator describes Marlow as an inveterate searcher, eager
   to go to little-known places, eager to unearth underlying
   truths as well; his restlessness separates him from most people, who lead narrow, cautious lives, and provides him with the
   daring to make the Congo trip. (Marlow himself explains his actions by saying that he felt he <u>had</u> to go to the Congo, im-
   pelled by some indefinable, unknowable force.)

2. If we see Kurtz as an exceptionally gifted product of Western
   civilization and if we believe the jungle represents the world
   we all inhabit (Conrad--as well as Marlow--seems to want us to
   make those connections), then we must conclude from this story
   that our brutal environment often acts as a catalyst on an evil
   we all carry within us. And although it's possible to escape
   corruption, an escape dependent upon rigorous honesty and
   strength, the overall tone of the story is wholeheartedly
   pessimistic.

3. Kurtz is a deliberately "flat" character. Because we are left
   guessing about his background and motivations, we are invited
   to project our own assumptions onto the blank surface of his
   character, making Kurtz's horror all the more personal for us.

4. On a functional level, the character of the Russian helps to
   propel the story: he provides Marlow (and the reader) with
   some information on Kurtz's power and decline. On a more symbolic level, the Russian shows that innocence, good intentions,
   and energy are not effective defenses against moral decay;
   the Russian is good-hearted but simple and unreflective, and so
   falls under Kurtz's sway.

5. Marlow allows the Intended's illusions about Kurtz's devotion
   and goodness to live because he believes that most people--and
   women especially--are not equipped to bear the truth about the
   pervasiveness of evil in the world. Marlow's lie is a partly
   compassionate, partly condescending attempt to prolong the woman's false but comfortable existence.

6. Heart of Darkness abounds with symbolism: each character, each
   descriptive passage, and each incident function as a symbol.
   To use one broad example, the central action of the story is,
   simply put, a journey through a jungle, but Conrad does not
   allow the story to exist only on this anecdotal level. He carefully leads us away from a superficial interpretation, allowing
   us to see the journey as a symbol for our trek through life
   and—further—as a symbol for introspection into our own hearts.

7. Marlow undertakes his journey to the Congo with great enthusiasm
   and vitality, and returns with a Buddha-like remove, a transfor-
   mation suggesting a heightened awareness and a subsequent renun-
   ciation of worldly activity.

POETRY

INTRODUCTION

1. The first five lines of Williams's "Young Woman at a Window"
describe the young woman; then, after exactly half of the poem
the poet shifts to the second of the two figures, the child.
The last half depicts him. The poet has created a careful sym-
metry in which there is a mirrorlike effect, the child mirror-
ing the young woman, even though both are behind the glass.
There are five lines apiece for the young woman and for the
child, twelve and eleven words, respectively, which might
suggest that the young woman is hardly more than a child herself, especially at this traumatic time.

2. In describing the unnaturalness of war, Wilfred Owen focuses on
a young boy in "Arms and the Boy" to illustrate the dichotomy
between the viciousness of armed conflict and the boy's inher-
ent soft and loving nature. The rhymes are forceful one-
syllable rhymes, called masculine rhymes, and consistently are
imperfect: for example, blade/blood. Their jarring lack of
compatibility corresponds to the lack of congruity between the
boy and the cold, impersonal instruments of war, and by extension, the general disregard for individual humanity manifested
by military organizations. The rhyming technique thus reinforces the message of the poem in a beautifully patterned way
that plainly says war is inhuman.

3. Giovanni's "Poem for Flora" centers on the aspirations, which
most people have, to be more attractive, more renowned and es-
teemed, more powerful (or at least more in control of themselves and of their lives). The glamour of being in the lime-
light, as the Queen of Sheba undoubtedly was while visiting
Solomon's court, is a common desire in people of all ages and
races. These aspirations often manifest themselves in a form
of hero-worship such as the child exhibits in this poem.

4. The speaker in Levertov's "The Secret" comes to know that the
human spirit not only yearns to know the secret of life (and
of death, lines 25-26), but gains delight and deep satisfaction
in searching for the secret. A strong implication is that for
those who make the effort to search, sudden (3) revelations
will come, insights somewhat mystical or inexplicable; the
poet, for example, missed the insight the two girls gained, even
though she wrote the line of poetry that provided the insight.
Another readily apparent implication is that because those who

discover life's secret quickly forget what it was, yet are able (if they search) to rediscover it repeatedly, "a thousand times, till death" (25), the secret must be discoverable and understandable only through extrarational faculties.

5. Baraka, like Owen in "Arms and the Boy," presents us with a stark contrast between the generally serene world of the young and the turbulent world of the adult. His speaker, obviously distressed, pessimistic about the world, and unable to discover answers to life's problems, suddenly encounters his (or her) daughter at prayer, speaking to the Creator of the stars that the parent counts but does not understand. The apparent insight of the speaker is that the child is far better off, and further that her simple faith might lead the parent to a more positive, healthy outlook.

6. A raw experience is portrayed in Frost's "Out, Out--", almost too harsh and realistic for a successful poem. Emotions in the poem include serenity, peace (lines 1-6); satisfaction of work, yet relief when work is finished (7-12); grim humor (19); horror, fear, consternation, and shock (18-31); and resignation and acceptance of death (33-34). We sense that these emotions are depicted in a genuine, realistic, and truthful manner partly because no one, including the speaker, appears to be pretending, covering up, falsifying, or making light of the situation. The speaker is frank in portraying the doctor as emotionally uninvolved, the family as hardy and accustomed to calamity, apparently hiding their deeper feelings behind daily chores.

CHAPTER 8   DENOTATION AND CONNOTATION

Raymond Carver

PHOTOGRAPH OF MY FATHER IN HIS TWENTY-SECOND YEAR

1. The actual setting for this poem involves only one person, the
   speaker. Most likely male, the speaker appears to be alone in
   a damp, "unfamiliar kitchen," which suggests a shiftless life-
   style. His thoughtful description of the photograph of his
   father reveals him to be a sensitive, perceptive person; his
   attempt to blame his father, at least in part, for what he has
   become depicts him as a person trying to escape responsibility
   for his own life. Equally unattractive is the almost maudlin
   self-pity we sense at the poem's conclusion. In comparing himself to his father at twenty-two, the speaker in the last two
   lines also implies that he is about the same age.

2. The speaker/son is attempting to communicate his disappointment
   in his father for neglecting to teach him to fish (probably for
   neglecting him in general) and for bequeathing to him a taste
   and a weakness for liquor instead. The son, who in this vi-
   gnette tacitly evaluates himself, is also critical of his father
   for being false, for pretending to be something he was not, not
   only in posing "bluff and hearty" for the snapshot but in life
   itself.

3. This poem is useful for leading students to look carefully at
   the printed word. Dank denotes unpleasant dampness. Sheepish
   suggests sheeplike, and several common associations with sheep
   are apparent: the father looks embarrassed, or foolish and
   silly like a sheep; he tries to appear bold, but (like a sheep)
   lacks fortitude, courage, initiative. The Latin preposition
   circa, meaning about or around, is readily understandable because it connects car and date. The denotation of bluff
   (rough; blunt but kindly) can be ascertained from the word's
   obvious connection with hearty, a more familiar word meaning
   cordial, vigorous, healthy. Too, the descriptions following
   bluff (8-9) provide assistance in defining the word by creating
   a picture of the father's bluff appearance. The perceptive
   student might notice that although bluff is here an adjective,
   the meaning of bluff as a verb (to deceive by putting on a bold
   front) is also appropriate to the situation; hence the father,
   in trying to be bluff, is bluffing.

40

4. The <u>dank</u> kitchen implies that the scene is near a waterfront, probably in a cheap or run-down dwelling. <u>Sheepish</u> grin aligns the father with the unthinking crowd rather than showing him to be the assertive individual the speaker wishes he was. <u>Bluff and hearty</u>, which the father pretends to be but is not, helps convey the theme of deception, which is especially meaningful as it relates to the speaker, who is a failure like his father (certainly partly because of his father) and perhaps posing as a <u>bluff and hearty</u> poet.

5. The poem is effective and memorable partly because it focuses on only two examples of ties between son and father--fishing and drinking, which are themselves closely related in the snapshot--thus keeping the picture a simple and unified one. Further, the poem deals with elementary principles in parent-child relationships that most readers readily recognize.

John Crowe Ransom

BELLS FOR JOHN WHITESIDE'S DAUGHTER

1. The situation can be summarized as follows: the speaker who uses the plural <u>we</u> meaning, apparently, a neighboring couple, is more sophisticated than the ordinary farm couple, judging by the speakers' diction. At the moment of the poem, they are at a house, presumably John Whiteside's, looking at his daughter "primly propped" (20) for burial, as the bells of a nearby church begin to toll, ostensibly announcing services for the girl. The import of the poem is the speakers' surprise at the active girl's stillness.

<u>Brown study</u> denotes a state of reverie or deep thought (here, death); <u>bruited</u>, talked about; <u>harried</u>, harassed; <u>scuttling</u>, scurrying; <u>vexed</u>, puzzled, annoyed.

2. <u>Wars</u>, childhood games; <u>arms</u>, gesticulated with her arms; <u>snow</u>, loose feathers; <u>goose</u>, goose-talk; <u>rod</u>, stick.

3. The Whiteside's daughter, perhaps about five or six years old, has been seen by the speakers playing outdoors with such vigor that her contrasting inertness in death so <u>astonishes</u> them that they can scarcely express their feelings. Perhaps their amazement masks deeper emotions--sadness, vexation over the death of an innocent child, fear of their own approaching deaths.

Because the first and last stanzas are connected by the repeated phrase her <u>brown study</u> (3, 19) and the astonishment and vexation felt by the onlookers, and because the first stanza refers to <u>us all</u>, including mourners in addition to the speakers, the final stanza is logically read as depicting a group viewing the body immediately prior to the funeral service.

Phyllis McGinley

INTIMATIONS OF MORTALITY

1. <u>Querulous</u>, whining (usually with reference to a complaining person); <u>anguish</u>, excruciating pain (most often meaning mental
pain, but here physical pain); <u>charily</u>, sparingly, carefully;
<u>oblivion</u>, a state of forgetfulness after death; <u>apprenticed</u>,
bound for a set period (in this case, to oblivion); <u>shrewd</u>, art-
ful, sagacious.

2. <u>Narrow anguish</u> means pain limited in at least two ways: localized and of short duration.

3. The dentist's admonition is expressed in the epigraph ("This
will be over soon"). The speaker-patient's reply, unspoken to
the dentist, is carried in lines 19-20, and points to the inexorable truth that time passes.

4. The speaker-patient clearly has the upper hand. The dentist's
control is a <u>narrow</u> one, localized and short. He is powerless
to keep the patient in pain forever.

William Shakespeare

SONNET 12

1. Direct or indirect references to time can be found in every line
except line 9. The cumulative effect of all these indications
of the passage of time is to cause the speaker to consider how
to prevent Time's victory over living things.

2. In this context and time period, <u>breed</u> as a noun could denote
posterity. The speaker concludes that only through having
children and subsequent descendents can the person addressed in
line 9 preserve his or her beauty.

3. According to the <u>OED</u>, <u>brave</u> as an adjective (line 2) could denote someone "splendid, showy, grand, fine, handsome" (see the
first boldface entry for <u>brave</u>, Sense A [adj], 2); also, someone having "the superabundance of any valuable quality" (Sense
A, 3). In Shakespeare's poem, the "brave day sunk in hideous
night" (line 2) is the first reference to Time's destructive
power; even more than the images that follow, <u>brave day</u> represents the person in line 9. Consequently, using the adjective
<u>brave</u> to denote the sun's brilliance, vigor, and beauty is to
select nature's most vital element as a symbol of the beauty of
the person whose aging is the poet's theme.

John Lennon and Paul McCartney

SHE'S LEAVING HOME

1. This lonely girl still feels emotionally attached to and dependent on her home, even though it has lacked the warmth we normally associate with a <u>home</u>. If the dwelling were merely a <u>house</u> to her, she would not regret or fear leaving it.

2. The parental responses connote self-effacing sacrifice--"We never thought of ourselves," (17), but in reality their devotion to their daughter has been misdirected. Note, for example, that the parents claim to have given their daughter "most of our lives" (mentioned twice in line 7), drawing attention to what they themselves have missed and given up because of their daughter. But we learn what aspect of their lives they have sacrificed--"everything money could buy" (7), which they now may realize failed to contain the <u>fun</u> (23) that every person craves.

The mother's reference to her daughter as "our baby" (14) connotes the parents' view of her as an immature girl requiring protection and supervision. Calling her "our girl" or "our daughter" would suggest that the parents consider her more grown-up. Calling her by name would connote a closer relationship than actually exists. Calling her "that sneak" would connote a sour relationship; the girl certainly has felt confined and discontented, but her parents appear to have been largely unaware of her feelings.

3. Parental selfishness is readily apparent in the following: their immediate focus on what <u>they</u> have done for her (7, 17); their proud claim to have sacrificed so much for her (7, 17); the mother's first outburst, focused on herself ("How could she treat us so thoughtlessly/How could she do this to me," 15, 16); their self-pity ("We struggled all our lives to get by," 17); and their inability to see how they could do anything wrong in raising a daughter (23).

Their daughter appears to leave home chiefly because of "something inside that was always denied/For so many years" (24-25), namely the opportunity to have a good time (23). Thus her parents do not appear to be overly cruel; and she, in turn, respects them at least enough to leave a note "that she hoped would say more" than she could say face to face (3). She flees an apparently cold and repressive home for what purports to be an attractive world of affection from and fun with a "man from the motor trade." Certainly parental selfishness is at the heart of the problem, yet the girl also exhibits considerable selfishness in leaving the home so abruptly.

Nikki Giovanni

A POEM FOR CAROL

1. Familiar connotations: red ribbons, the delights of wrapped
   gifts, especially those at Christmas (red and green traditionally being associated with that season); lincoln heights, the
   first word connoting Abraham Lincoln as the emancipator of black
   America, the second word connoting a fashionable suburb--which
   this area is not--hence drawing attention to the contrast between aspirations ("heights") for and of black Americans and
   the realities, such as the lack of sidewalks in Lincoln Heights;
   sewer connotes the sordid, unpleasant sides of life, the harsh,
   smelly realities (which the speaker bravely asserts were not
   really too bad, 6); little kitten connotes innocent, defenseless, and beautiful living creatures--including people.

2. Carol (n.) denotes a song of religious joy or mirth, nearly always associated with Christmas; carol (v.) denotes joyful out-
   door singing at Christmas. The two words connote the emotions
   associated with this holiday--family love, security, acceptance,
   compassion for others, the delights of giving gifts, and religious joys. These denotations and connotations appear appropriate to the poem, especially given the apparent associations with
   Christmas carried by red ribbons, not only because a family situation is involved, but because the kitten is a sort of anonymous gift to the speaker that moves her deeply. Also, the dis-
   figured, innocent kitten could easily be taken as a generalized
   symbol of the crucified Christ who emerged, like the kitten,
   from the earth; seemingly more apt for an Easter poem, this
   interpretation carries credence when one considers that the
   kitten might represent the infant Jesus, thus rendering the
   poem a commentary on the bittersweet nature of the Nativity.

3. The speaker's point of view is that of a child. Because the
   one-eyed kitten impresses the child deeply, we are secure in
   concluding that the child, the sister, and gary are sensitive
   to the poignancy the kitten embodies. Further, the fact that
   the kitten becomes the cause of a deep experience for the speaker, touching to her (or him) even years later when the experience is told in verse, leads us to believe that the speaker as
   a child was unusually sensitive and perceptive: for example,
   "i knew / i had nothing to give that would / replace her one
   gone eye" (20-22).

Carol Lynn Pearson

OF PLACES FAR

For most readers, the Blue Mosque will connote mysterious, unfamiliar religious rites. The speaker appears to share with us
these feelings about Middle Eastern religion: Istanbul is "only
a name." His or her feelings about Istanbul change to more

familiar ones after the speaker visits the city and the mosque
vicariously through a friend or relative. Heaven is even more re-
mote and unfamiliar, but the speaker comes to know something of it
through the same vicarious method as that involved with Istanbul.

Claude McKay

THE WHITE HOUSE

Vitals, vital organs, and by extension, the inner person or soul;
chafing, discontented; wrathful, filled with vengeful anger, indignation; inviolate, pure and undefiled.

1. "The White House" suggests the residence of the U.S. President,
   and it might be taken to mean all that the Washington mansion
   symbolizes. In addition, it suggests "white houses" in gen-
   eral--that is, any domicile, business, club, or organization
   that excludes people on the basis of race (or any other basis).
   The poet, in his autobiography A Long Way from Home (1937), excludes both of these interpretations and suggests certain (but
   not all) "white houses" that because of deadly hate exclude
   blacks.

   Evidence against interpreting the white house as the President's residence can be found in the phrase the decent street
   (line 7), connoting a residential area rather than downtown
   Washington. The shuttered door of glass might appear contradictory, however, as it connotes a business establishment. Possibly the poem suggests both. The final six lines speak of
   generalized feelings, laws, hatreds, thereby implying that the
   speaker refers not to a single, specific white house, but to
   many.

2. Both this poem and Blake's "A Poison Tree" focus on the effects
   of human hatred, and both liken that hatred to poison. In
   Blake's poem, the speaker's foe is killed by a disguised wrath;
   in McKay's, the speaker is the potential victim, struggling to
   keep from being poisoned by a hatred that is only thinly disguised.

3. This exercise calls for a personal response.

John Milton

ON THE LATE MASSACRE IN PIEDMONT

1. Milton's passionate indignation is expressed in the following:
   calling the event a massacre, a slaughter, a slaying, a martyrdom; calling God to avenge the deed; emphasizing the atrocities (scattering of bones over the cold mountainside; the
   groans; the bloody hands of the slayers; the mother with an

infant thrown down the cliffs); and the indictment of the triple Tyrant (or the Pope, with his three-tiered crown).

2. Substitutions might be extermination for massacre, slaughter, slaying, and martyrdom; praising God for the successful rid-dance; omission of the atrocities, particularly the incident with the mother and infant; and examples of valiant conflicts won against the 'dissidents.'

William Butler Yeats

THE LAKE ISLE OF INNISFREE

1. Among the literal images are these: small cabin...of clay and
   wattles, bean rows, beehive, and glade. Among the figurative
   images are peace that comes dropping slow, veils of the morning,
   midnight that is all a glimmer, noon that is a purple glow,
   evening that is full of the linnet's wings.

2. Sound is expressed or implied in many images, including building the cabin, beehive, bee-loud glade, peace, cricket singing,
   sound of the linnet's wings, lake water lapping...by the shore
   and heard in the deep heart's core. Touch is expressed or implied in these images (among others): clay (slipperiness),
   wattles (roughness), honey (stickiness), wings (softness).
   Taste appears in the references to beans, honey, and water.

3. The island he longs for is described more vividly. At present
   the speaker is in the city (pavements grey).

Paul Vesey (Samuel W. Allen)

IN MY FATHER'S HOUSE

1. The speaker generally employs figurative imagery to describe
   his fear. Examples: the falling of dusk (line 1), the pan-
   ther night (10), the bound of the speaker's heart (11, 22), the
   feet refusing to move (12-13), the power lurking (17-18), the
   weapons in the speaker's hand (24), the cold grey waves stif-
   ling and drowning him (27-28). Samples of literal imagery:
   house, first floor, outer door, and so forth.

2. In general, Vesey's imagery is fairly fixed: the speaker presumably is male, suggested by the throwing of "the ball the
   stone the spear in my hand" (24); the approximate time of day
   is specified, as are several details of the house. But the
   imagery used to describe the "power" is very free; this vague-
   ness works to make the assualt more terrible by giving it a
   nightmarish, incomprehensible quality.

POETRY

3. Among many sensory images are the following: sound (bolting and locking the doors and their opening quietly, the imagined throwing of the objects at the house, the <u>waves</u>); touch (<u>earthen floor</u>); temperature (<u>cold waves</u>); distance (the presence of the house, the doors, the yard, the ground); movement (the closing and opening of the doors, the bounding of the heart, the entrance of the <u>power</u>, the rushing of the speaker into the yard).

John Keats

THIS LIVING HAND

1. This appears to be a poem of unrequited love. The speaker, presumably male, assures his beloved that if he dies of heartache, he (in the image of his hand), as well as her own conscience, will haunt and torment her for rejecting him.

2. Imagery associated with the hand in this poem includes the sense of being alive (<u>this living hand</u>) contrasted with being dead (lines 2-6); temperature (<u>warm hand</u>, 1; <u>cold</u> and <u>icy</u> hand, 2-3, that can <u>chill</u> one's <u>nights</u>, 4); pressure (<u>grasping</u> hand, 2); hearing (the hand in the <u>silence of the tomb</u>, 3); wetness and circulation of blood (6), contrasting with the dryness of a dead heart (5), and both with reference to blood giving life to the hand; and finally, movement of the hand (8).

3. The vividness and wide range of imagery save the poem from a debilitating self-pity. Because the relationship described is one-sided, the expression of self-pity at first strikes us as both immature and melodramatic: "You'll regret what you've done to me!" Yet the alternating contrasts between life and death, warmth and cold, pulsing and stillness have an effective influence on our sensibilities, enabling us to feel the vibrant nature of a living person seeking affection, and through this means helping us to realize how delicate the threads of life and love are.

Keats's methods of evoking emotional response are his references to traditional imagery of romantic love: the grasping of hands, the warmth of physical contact, the chill of rejection, and the heart; and his heavy reliance on the hand as an image of invitation, friendship, loyalty, covenants and marriage vows --all connoting security and acceptance.

William Butler Yeats

THE SONG OF WANDERING AENGUS

1. Yeats uses gold (or yellow) and silver (or white). These two colors, expressed or implied, occur as follows: <u>fire</u> (yellow, 2), <u>white moths</u> (5), <u>moth-like stars</u> (6), <u>silver trout</u> (8),

48

fire (10), apple blossom (white, 14), brightening air (yellow, 16), old (white, 17), silver apples (23), moon (23), golden apples (24), and the sun (24). The image pattern is an alternating one, from gold to silver, suggesting (on one level) the cycles of time experienced by the speaker, from day to night, youth to age.

2. The speaker pursues an imaginary lover, one conjured from his own brain by a wand (3). The silver imagery pertains to the nocturnal (and largely imaginary) experience of stanzas 1 and 2; the poet employs this imagery to describe the magical, the imaginary. The gold imagery refers to the speaker's passion, the "fire" that burns within him. The final fusion of the two colors might be seen as an attempt to suggest that Aengus has become incapable of distinguishing between the imaginary and the real. The two colors make the poem an ever-changing scintillation representing the imbalance caused by love.

Also, "golden apples of the sun" is a probable allusion to one of the nearly impossible twelve tasks of Hercules, that of obtaining the Golden Apples of Hesperides, daughter of Atlas. Hercules holds up the world while Atlas gets the apples, but then finds he must trick Atlas into taking the world back. In Yeats's poem, the old man faces a similarly difficult task.

3. Aengus is now an old man, yet still obsessed with the beauty and sexual potential of the imaginary "glimmering girl" he claims to have seen in a youthful vision. He has become mentally imbalanced, like the lover in "Lost Love," who believes his senses have been heightened to a superhuman level by grief over unfulfilled love. Browning's male speaker is also absorbed by passion, and he too displays a heightened sensibility; but because his love is soon to be consummated, we presume that he and his lover will regain their normal perspective, at least by morning. Keats's speaker is consumed by passion enough to project fantasies as well; however, he vows to return as a ghost to haunt his would-be lover for failure to return his affections, thus becoming in a sense a demon, seeking revenge.

Gwendolyn Brooks

kitchenette building

1. The poem appeals most strongly to the senses of smell (onion fumes, fried potatoes, yesterday's garbage, bathroom), hearing (giddy sound, sing an aria), and touch (cooking, warm it, lukewarm water).

2. The speaker might at first appear to be singular and female because of the references to cooking and a domestic life, and because the poet is female. Yet the first pronoun (we, line 1) is plural, the first clearly differentiated point of view is male (feeding a wife, 3), and the next point of view is female

(satisfying a man, 3). Because the speakers are all in the kitchenette building, are grayed in and gray, having involuntary
plans, cooking, thinking of singing, waiting for the use of a
shared bathtub down the hall, we assume the speakers are female.
Details in the poetic picture reveal them to be middle-aged or
older, musical, accustomed to shelving occasional dreams in favor of daily necessities, and on the low-income level. The
poem conveys their unfulfilled desire to escape from the dreary
facts of their everyday life into the world of their dreams.

3. The first and last lines tell us that these speakers move con-
tinuously through the same daily cycle of tasks and activities,
from dry (and in need of a bath) to wet (and clean), from hun-
gry to satisfied, and so forth. They have dreams of finer
things--of dance ("flutter...down these rooms," 7), of singing
(7), from which they might obtain a message (10), but they are
too poor to pursue dreams. In other words, they would like to
keep their dreams warm and clean, but are forced to concentrate
their energy on keeping their bodies warm and clean instead.

Andrew Marvell

BERMUDAS

A noticeable image cluster--in this case, of tropical fruits--is
contained in lines 17-24. An image pattern can be observed in the
reiterated references to God, which unify the description of the
isle as well as provide a visual and auditory reinforcement of
the rowing movements. Another image pattern is apparent in the
tour of the island that the hymn provides: from ocean to the
shore, to the air, the trees, the ground, the trees, back to the
shore, then (by implication) beyond the isle back upon the ocean.
This is a completed cycle, typical of Renaissance attention to
form.

James Thomson

from WINTER

1. Most of the images are fixed. The poet wishes us to "see," to
"feel," and in general to "sense" the reality of the scene and
the experience.

2. Among the negative images that connote various fears are the
following: Winter (line 2); the dark (2); the sense of being
in a trackless, unmarked, formless terrain (6-8); despair and
horror (14) at being deceived by the snowdrifts; night (19);
wind (20-21); the wilderness (21); the pits (23), bogs (25),
cliffs (25), and lake (28) hidden by snow; the sensation of
sinking (30-31); death (32); cold seizing the nerves, senses,

and <u>vitals</u> (42–44). These images convey fear of the unknown, of being lost, and of death.

3. Nearly all the fears relate to the senses.

CHAPTER 10   FIGURATIVE LANGUAGE

D. H. Lawrence

BABY RUNNING BAREFOOT

1. Similes: feet "like white flowers in a wind" (2), "like puffs
   of wind" (3), "winsome as a robin's song (6), "like two butterflies" (7), and "cool as syringa buds . . . or firm and silken
   as young peony flowers" (13-14); and baby moving "like a wind-
   shadow" (10). The similes not only render the baby and its
   white feet more vivid and memorable, but they also draw the baby
   into harmony with the delicate world of nature around it.

2. The common denominator is the delicate in nature--the child's
   feet are compared to flowers, wind, a robin's song, butterflies,
   flower buds, and young flowers.

3. Tack, to change direction; syringa buds, buds of the genus Phil-
   adelphus, ornamental shrubs with creamy-white and strongly
   scented flowers (OED); peony flowers, any of the genus Paeonia,
   having large flowers of red, pink, or white. The poet relies on
   connotations of softness, delicacy, sweetness, innocence, and
   purity in his imagery, which are especially appropriate for the
   baby in his poem.

George Herbert

THE WINDOWS

1. A minister, like a stained-glass window, is full of cracks and
   flaws, yet he occupies a place of importance, through which
   God's teachings (like light) pass to His children.

2. A good preacher is one who, apparently because of personal
   worthiness and the grace of God (5), is a richly colored conduit
   of God's light; the story of God he conveys to the congregation,
   like a biblical scene in stained glass, will be ample in "doc-
   trine and life, colors and light" (11). A weak preacher, in
   contrast, lacks within himself the "light and glory" (8); thus,
   the message he delivers, the picture he presents, "shows water-
   ish, bleak,& thin" (10). His sermon is "speech alone [which] /
   Doth vanish like a flaring thing, / And in the ear, not conscience ring" (13-15).

FIGURATIVE LANGUAGE

3. Conceits in Donne's "A Valediction: Forbidding Mourning": the parting of true lovers is like the parting at death of soul and body in a _virtuous_ man--peaceful, confident (stanzas 1 and 2); it is also like the "trepidation of the spheres," a gigantic motion of heavenly bodies more tremulous than earthquakes, yet harmless (stanza 3); it is like an expansion of the two lovers, rather than a break between them--like beaten gold (stanza 6); and it is like the parting of two compass feet, joined at the top, the traveling foot kept true and faithful by the fixed foot (stanzas 7-9).

Molly Holden

GIANT DECORATIVE DAHLIA

1. The dahlia shows the toughness and determination of individuals (or animals, plants) who succeed despite incredible odds. When the flower turns "its great innocent face . . . triumphantly" toward the speaker (15-17), it becomes personified, and the speaker loves it as though it were a person (18).

2. Holden's personification derives much of its effectiveness from the emphasis on the dahlia bulb's being _unnamed_ and _offered cheap_ (6), yet in the end outclassing all the "colored heads and steady stems" (4) in the garden. The implication is that the bulb is like an orphan (_unnamed_) or a child deemed worthless, unpromising, weak, or who is handicapped, but who triumphs in adulthood.

Owen's personifications are more complex, evoking human characteristics in nonhuman objects that take on aspects partly human, partly bestial: bayonet-blade steel "keen with hunger of blood" (2), _blue with malice_ like that of a _madman_ (3), and a cannibal famished for human _flesh_ (4); _bullet-heads_ that _long to nuzzle_ in lads' hearts (6), a hint of romantic love, but with overtones of murderous seduction; ammunition with _zinc teeth_, _sharp_ with human _grief and death_ (8). The final stanza demonstrates that the boy is no beast, but war would turn him into one, and would kill him as well.

Keats's ode is replete with personification, among which are these: the _urn_ is likened to a virgin _bride_ (1), a _foster child_ (2), a _historian_ (3); _boughs_ are called _happy_ (21); a _little town_ is _silent_ and _desolate_ (38-40); the urn, which "dost tease us out of thought" (44) speaks (48-49). The effectiveness of Keats's personification can be sensed in the delight we feel in encountering each vestige of human life and activity on an inanimate (and _cold_, 45) object which conveys a sense of real human scenes, acts, and emotions.

William Wordsworth

LINES WRITTEN IN EARLY SPRING

The poet's point is that the plants and creatures of nature enjoy their existence and share an established harmony. In contrast, human beings have taught, led, or caused one another to be discontented or dissatisfied with their existence; they lack the harmony found in nature.

Carmen Tafolla

SAN ANTONIO

1. Presently the speaker is addressing the city. In the past, people addressing it have been those unable (or unwilling) to understand the Mexican-Americans of the city.

2. San Antonio, in the poem, is its Chicano population. It has been judged "lazy" because it has been different and misunderstood--e.g., silent (3), given to singing in the night (7), and soft-hearted (12). The speaker's tone and the statement in line 14 (the non-Chicano population saw, 10, but didn't [really] see nor understand, 14, indicate rejection of this judgment, and the imagery implies that the speaker finds the Chicano people of San Antonio beautiful and strong.

3. The imagery appeals to the sense of hearing, but is curiously muted, possibly in keeping with the silence mentioned in line 3: silent, subtle, screaming eyes (3); centuries-secret sweet-night song (7); mute bell-toll (11); river-ripple heart (12); sigh on strife (13). Imagery also appeals to the sense of sight, specifically to objects relating to bright sunshine: bronzed workmaid's arms (5); skybirth and sunaltar (10); corn-dirt soul (11). The imagery is unified by the repetitive use of the words you and your.

4. Of the figures discussed to this point, the poem contains a covey of metaphors in the second stanza: the soul (or instinctive interests) related to corn-dirt; grief, to a mute bell-toll; the beat of the heart, to river-ripple[s]; an ancient shawl, to a sigh on strife. The first stanza contains examples of synecdoche, discussed later in this chapter: eyes, arms, singing voices represent the whole person, in this case the whole Chicano population of San Antonio.

Denise Levertov

SCENES FROM THE LIFE OF THE PEPPERTREES

1. The trees are like people in that they stand aside and express diffidence (5); they shiver (15; not solely human); one tree is

54

restless, twitching (40; not solely human); it <u>walks</u> to the house and <u>taps</u> on the window (43-44). The suggestion is that the trees can think like people. They are unlike people in their appearance, their inability to speak, and so forth.

Examples of the pathetic fallacy: the trees show <u>diffidence</u>; the sun is confident (13); the trees shudder a bit, as if fearful of impending events (15); the third tree is <u>restless</u> (40), eventually is unable to suppress its feelings, and taps a warning on an <u>upstairs window</u> (42ff.).

2. Cats and sun are unable to sense the imminent danger to the sleeping man; they are sure all is well. The trees are sensitive to the brewing trouble. Similarly sensitive trees and an insensitive cat appear in Anne Sexton's "Lament" ("Other Poems to Read").

3. Because the peppertrees sense the danger, the third tree attempts to wake the sleeping and defenseless man (32).

4. To warn the sleeping man. Peril is implicit not only in the uneasiness of the trees, but in the reference to "somebody / getting the hell / outta here" (26-28), and in the description of the man as completely vulnerable (32).

John Milton

from PARADISE LOST (BOOK IX)

Note: The lines from Book IX printed in this chapter have been renumbered for convenience (1-22), but in actuality are lines 412-433.

1. Eve is likened to the <u>fairest</u> flower in Paradise (21), Adam to her support or <u>prop</u> (22) of <u>myrtle</u> vine (20).

2. Eve's morning task, binding up the tall flowers whose heads <u>hung drooping unsustained</u> (19), emphasizes that the beauties of the paradisal Garden are more splendid when supported and sustained by companion plants--in this case, <u>myrtle</u>. We are prepared, thus, for the central metaphor of Eve as the fairest flower: she too, by extension, is most resplendent, fulfilled, and secure against the impending storm (22) when Adam, her support, is near. Elsewhere in Book IX Milton points out that Adam also is more secure against the storm (or Satan) when Eve is near: in Adam's own words, "each / To other speedy aid might lend at need" (259-260), and "I from the influence of thy looks receive / Access in every virtue, in thy sight [that is, when we are together] / More wise, more watchful, stronger" (309-11; see also 370-372, wherein Adam says that <u>both</u> of them are less careful when alone).

Eve is like a flower not only in physical beauty and in her corresponding power to enthrall, uplift, and inspire; she is like

a primal flower in her role as mother of the human race, the
potential source of all human seeds or posterity. Adam is like
a band or vine of myrtle in a semiliteral sense: he provides
physical strength to protect and support the supple flower; in
addition, he functions as a figurative support to Eve, just as
she does for him--as the vine, he relies on the flower stalk for
support even as he helps support it.

3. Milton presents Adam and Eve as types of all men and women.
   They are inherently obedient and innocent, yet they display imperfections (even before the Fall) that render them vulnerable
   to deception and error. They make mistakes, feel ashamed and
   worthless, but are able to persevere by learning from their er-
   rors what to avoid, and in a religious context) hearkening to
   the counsels of their Maker.

Langston Hughes

THE WEARY BLUES

1. The rhythm is definite and easily discernible, especially when
   the poem is read aloud.

2. The rhythm of "The Weary Blues" is not as regular or as repetitive as that of a nursery rhyme, for example, but the cadence is
   there, underpinning the poem. The musical portions--lines within the quotation marks--are more regular than the rest of the
   poem.

3. The juxtaposition of stressed and unstressed syllables provides
   the basis for the rhythm of this and other poems. Here, however, Hughes adds a dimension--the conventions of blues music.
   The song portion of the poem brings to mind traditional blues
   music with its own particular timing and rests, as well as the
   drawing out of certain syllables.

A. E. Housman

R. L. S.

Henry David Thoreau

HAZE

1. The stresses in "R. L. S." occur in regular but varying patterns. The slack syllables, too, are regular.

2. In "R. L. S." the accents fall at regular intervals and the alternating lines are of the same length--eight syllables in
   lines 1, 3, 5, 7, 9, and 11, and six syllables in lines 2, 4, 6,
   8, 10, and 12. In "Haze" the accents are not regular and the
   lines are of various lengths. Here again, reading aloud will
   help establish which poem has the more regular meter.

3. The whole point of Thoreau's poem is to give a description of
   the haze of an ephemeral, drifting ocean, sun-glancing, lazy,

and serene. Clearly, the lack of a strong, regular beat is compatible with this idea; the poem stands as a fine example of how theme and metrical structure can work together to make a harmonious, organic whole work of art.

George Gordon, Lord Byron

THE DESTRUCTION OF SENNACHERIB

1. The meter is anapestic tetrameter.

2. The da-da-DA, da-da-DA of the anapestic line helps to suggest the beating of horses' hooves on the hard-packed earth. Again, the meter directly relates to the subject matter of the poem; the result is a harmony between structure and meaning.

3. The simile in the last line of the fourth stanza sets up a comparison between the foam and the last gasps of the horse and the spray of surf. The suggestion is that the regular beating of sea against shore is as inexorable as the working out of the Divine Will; the metrical pattern reinforces the idea of eternal rhythm and the weakness of the "mighty" in the face of God and time.

Thomas Wyatt

IF THOU WILT MIGHTY BE

1. The meter is iambic pentameter.

2. There are several variations to the meter; for example, lines 2, 7, 8, 9, and 11. Variation is used here to preserve the meaning of the poem and to avoid artificiality. Because the meter is not so intricately tied to the meaning of the poem as is the meter in a work such as "The Destruction of Sennacherib," the variations do not detract from the work.

William Carlos Williams

QUEEN-ANN'S-LACE

1. To some extent, the question of whether regular meter enhances a poem involves personal opinion. The beauty and workmanship of this poem are, of course, obvious, and one would be hard put to show how Williams could have improved it.

2. The poem includes internal rhythms, though they are not regular, perhaps, and not obvious. See, for example, lines 7 and 16. Compare the language of this poem to that of any of the

selections in the fiction section. It will become apparent why
free verse is real poetry and not just lines of prose.

Gerard Manley Hopkins

THE WINDHOVER

1. Hopkins's meter is not free because it involves a regular number of stressed syllables to every line; no matter what the total number of syllables is. Note that line 1 is perfect iambic
pentameter.

2. The question of whether sprung rhythm is "too sprung" is open
to discussion. Hopkins's poem is as rhythmic as a poem in free
verse, such as "Queen-Ann's-Lace," but it is not so metrically
regular as "The Destruction of Sennacherib." Reading Hopkins's
poetry aloud or listening to a recording of it is essential to
understanding how sprung rhythm works.

3. Hopkins, like many other great poets, often seems to choose a
word as much for its sound as for its meaning. The melody of
the line thus becomes as important as the rhythm, and this determines the way the line is organized.

A. E. Housman

"TERENCE, THIS IS STUPID STUFF"

1. The two speakers are friends who disagree because of the difference in the ways they deal with harsh reality. The first
speaker (stanza 1) prefers to ignore life's thorns; the second
speaker (stanzas 2, 3, and 4) would rather examine and write
about them.

2. Poison here symbolizes the various hardships we meet in life—
it's a given for all of us. Beer (and all other tricks that
fog reality, like silly poetry) is a temporary stopgap at best.
Thoughtful poetry, on the other hand, works as an effective an-
tidote to poison: by force-feeding us the truth little by little, it fortifies us for whatever rude shocks might come our
way.

Thomas Hardy

THE RUINED MAID

1. The speakers are two acquaintances from a rural district meeting
in town. One of the girls is "ruined," the other presumably
not. Obviously, no one speaks in regular anapestic couplets,

but the tone of this satiric-comic poem is light, and the very idea of two such persons speaking in verse is humorous.

2. Hardy purposely forces the meter at times, specifically in lines 3, 10, 15, and 19. This adds to the comic effect by stressing the unnaturalness of the speakers' dialogue.

3. Hardy is ridiculing the morality that condemns those who are sexually active outside of marriage, as the comparison of the "ruined" girl's condition before and after her "ruination" makes clear.

Emily Dickinson

I LIKE TO SEE IT LAP THE MILES--

1. The _it_ referred to in the first line is a railroad train. The central metaphor of the poem is the comparison of the train with a horse.

2. The meter is regular and slow at first, but then, around line 9, becomes less regular and faster. Toward the end of the poem, the meter, like the train, becomes more docile. Thus the meter, like the train and the horse, begins with a rhythmic chugging trot, breaks into a headlong, hooting gallop near the middle of the poem, and then slows to the regular gait of the beginning before stopping at the roundhouse door.

Henry Wadsworth Longfellow

THE TIDE RISES, THE TIDE FALLS

1. The sea-sands upon which the traveler hastens are the sands of time. The traveler, Everyperson, has his or her footprints erased because every mortal person lives (passes this way) only once.

2. Time is the milieu of mortal existence; since the theme of the poem is the transitory nature of human life, the first line of the poem is repeated three times to hammer home this point.

3. The meter, iambic tetrameter, is regular, like the ticking of a clock; it effectively suggests the inexorable march of time.

4. The tide's action suggests the inexorable ongoingness of life in the world, which does not notice the passing of any single individual.

Christina Rossetti

SONG

1. The lines in this poem are set up in pairs, suggesting the dual-
   ity of grief, remembering and forgetting.

2. Particular objects mentioned in the poem do contribute to the
   mood of melancholy. Rain, shadow, the shady tree, the twilight,
   and the nightingale all signify death, mourning, and a pensive
   moodiness. The mood that this poem evokes may be said to be
   contrived because it is not the actual plight of the speaker
   that we are likely to grieve for, but rather the situation as
   presented by the mention of sad songs, rain, etc. These objects
   act as signals designed to evoke emotions in and of themselves;
   the pathos we should feel for the speaker never really gets
   called up. Instead we are left with sentimentality.

3. The speaker in the poem sees death as a dreamlike state, apparently, in which the deceased exists in eternal twilight (see
   lines 13-14). In such an existence, the dead person is not
   able to see, feel, or hear (lines 9, 10, 11). It can be argued
   that such a view of death is a realistic one.

4. The speaker is in a melancholy mood, looking forward to a time
   when all of what this life has to offer is no longer available.
   Musing on mortality, the speaker's main concern seems to be
   that his or her own worldly existence is limited. This is the
   source of the melancholy.

Marnie Walsh

THE RED FOX

1. The meter is irregular, a condition that reinforces the speaker's sense of drifting and inconclusiveness.

2. The snow, the bus, the prairie, and the day itself are described
   as being grey, neither one thing nor another, uncertain. Pros-
   pects for the speaker seem equally uncertain; even the "road
   ahead/ real enough" leads only "somewhere." From the speaker's
   vantage point, in a world in which everything blends together,
   the red fox stands out, alone but singular in its identity.

3. The speaker seems to regard the fox with admiration and envy.
   The fox seems blessed, "sitting in his singular sunset," at
   peace with the elements and certain of his place in the world,
   while the observer travels in no apparent direction (line 9)
   over a trail on which landmarks are indistinct (line 13).

Matthew Arnold

DOVER BEACH

1. The thought brought forth in the sound is put forth in the next
   stanza. Arnold tells us that the sound of the sea reminds him
   that the Sea of Faith stands at ebb tide, withdrawn from the
   world. The problem the poem presents is what the individual is
   to do given the state of the modern world. The meter reinforces
   this idea with its weightiness and frequent pauses.

2. Sophocles long ago heard the roar of the withdrawing of meaning
   from life, the same sound that Arnold hears now. Cadence is
   rhythm or repetition; it plays an important part in this poem
   in that if faith, or meaning, is now in a state of withdrawal,
   we can be reasonably sure that the tide of truth and certainty
   is even now beginning to rise. The idea is more explicit at the
   end of Shelley's "Ode to the West Wind."

3. As Arnold describes it, the intellectual climate of the late
   nineteenth century was chaotic; religious tenets were seemingly
   at odds with scientific discoveries, social institutions struggled to adapt to new technologies, and political systems were
   attacked by revolutionary ideas. The poem suggests (in lines
   29 and 30) that personal relationships may help individuals
   survive this situation.

4. Lines 30-34 suggest that we are often lulled into complacency by
   a false sense of security. We need to see the world as it
   is, Arnold tells us, rather than as we might like it to be, before we can make decisions about how we are to live our lives.

Walt Whitman

BEAT! BEAT! DRUMS!

1. The poem is perhaps less metrically regular than others we have
   looked at, but no less rhythmic. Read the poem aloud.

2. Cadence, loosely termed, refers to rhythm rather than meter.
   Remember that meter is a regularized rhythm.

3. The drums and bugles represent the situations, persons, forces,
   and urges that bring on war.

Dylan Thomas

DO NOT GO GENTLE INTO THAT GOOD NIGHT

1. The speaker wants us to fight against death for as long as possible; in doing so, we assert our humanity and strength for one
last time.

2. The rhyme scheme is that of a villanelle: abaa.   The repeated
lines reinforce our perception of the inevitability of death
and underscore the speaker's plea.

3. The images of light in this poem are intense and largely active
images—"burn," "lightning," "bright," "sun," "blaze like me-
teors"—emphasizing that life is (or should be) a passionate,
energetic state. Death, a calm stasis, is "right," i.e., in-
evitable, but not to be welcomed.

Paula Gunn Allen

HOOP DANCER

1. It is hard for the modern observer to enter the world of American Indian belief, in which the interrelatedness of all
things—sky, water, Earth, the dancer's mind and body—is re-
garded as a basic truth.

2. Metrics are not irrelevant to the poem, but artificially imposed
rhythms are not relevant to the dance, the poem says, because
the dance produces its own metrics.

3. "Out of time" here means timeless, eternal, "beyond the march of
years."

POETRY

Alfred, Lord Tennyson

ULYSSES

1. The speaker seems to be addressing at least three audiences.
First, Ulysses speaks to his son, Telemachus, and explains his
reasons for leaving. Second, he introduces Telemachus to the
townspeople as their new king. Finally, Ulysses exhorts his
mariners to accompany him on this last adventure.

2. In the sense that Ulysses is refusing to live the life which has
been prescribed for him and that he insists on following his own
vision, he is heroic. On the other hand, he has traveled far
and wide, played a leading role in the events of his day, and is
as aged as his mate; perhaps it is unrealistic for him to expect
to be able to relive the old days.

3. Ulysses expects to find nothing after death except, perhaps,
sleep. This is one reason that he wishes to drink life to the
lees, to experience all he can in the time allotted him.

TITHONUS

1. The original intention of Eos and Tithonus was to preserve their
relationship just as it was, to make sure that it continued that
way throughout eternity. Their plan, of course, was thwarted by
the fact that Tithonus is granted eternal life but not eternal
youth. Change, then, enters into the relationship in the form
of aging, the nemesis of youthful love. Tithonus's position as
the lover of Eos is inexorably eroded as the hours take their
toll. He is doomed to watch each day dawn, bringing with it
both the pageant of Eos's beauty and the deterioration of his
own.

2. The goal of ordinance is the limit to which humans should
aspire.

3. Tithonus is being punished for his hubris, that prideful attitude which leads humans to press beyond mortal limits.

Geary Hobson

DEER HUNTING

1. The American Indians treat the deer as a gift from heaven, something to be treated with reverence and respect, while for the
white hunters the deer is a carcass to be hacked and mutilated.
For the Indians, the hunt is a part of the processes of nature;
the men, the deer, the dogs, and even the woods are participants
in an eternal chain of interrelated acts. The other hunters,
however, are not inclined to regard the event as anything more
than a singular event with no implications beyond the kill.

2. The diction, or word choice, of the two sets of hunters is important because it does help establish the attitudes and beliefs of the characters. The white hunters' speech is marked by profanity, while the Indian hunters' words are prayerlike. The actions involved in the dressing of the deer are contrasted, too, and give the reader clues as to the kinds of people being described. On the one hand the deer is handled gently, but on the other it is treated brutally and carelessly. Other clues to the contrasting ethos of the persons involved include the way the hunters treat one another.

3. The ritualistic elements in the second section are obvious: blood is smeared on the boy's face as a way of blessing him, the entrails are preserved, the raw liver is eaten as a token of homage to the deer's swiftness and strength, and part of the meat is returned to the woods. These are contrasted to the acts of the white hunters, which would be sacrilegious if they weren't so unthinking. Even the feeding of the dogs is part of the ritual for the Indian hunters; the corresponding action by the white group is hollow and sterile by comparison.

Theodore Roethke

THE WAKING

1. The poetic form is a villanelle, an intricate form consisting of five tercets, rhyming aba, followed by a quatrain rhyming abaa. Lines 6, 12, and 18 repeat line 1, and lines 9, 15, and 19 repeat line 3. This form helps the poet build on his ideas; it allows for a progression of thought. The form is appropriate to the theme in that Roethke is concerned in this poem with the entire cosmic process—growth, change, and progress—and with learning about this process.

2. The speaker's being can be heard, an indication that existence is tied closely to the senses. Being dances; the resultant metaphor is personification.

Percy Bysshe Shelley

ODE TO THE WEST WIND

1. The poem as a whole moves from the sense of death in the first stanza ("leaves dead," "like ghosts") to the sense of rejuvenation in the last stanza ("can Spring be far behind?"). The stanzaic pattern contributes to this progression in that each stanza is linked to the next by the rhyme; the b rhyme in each stanza becomes the a rhyme in the next.

2. The seasons of the year play an important part in the poem in that the progression of the seasons offers a metaphor for the cosmic process as seen by Shelley—a movement from life to

death to rebirth and hence to life again. The leaves and seeds of stanza 1, the clouds of stanza 2, and the sea of stanza 3 are the particulars to which Shelley turns his attention in his general statement on the cyclic nature of life.

3. The speaker wishes to be lifted out of mortal selfhood and to become like the wind, whose being touches all existence. If it is impossible to be elevated in this way, the speaker feels that he or she must suffer mortality.

Jonathan Swift

A DESCRIPTION OF A CITY SHOWER

1. The poem is realistic in that it describes the city the way it is, rather than the way we would perhaps like it to be. Swift's use of specific details, like the smell of the sewer, the dung, guts, and blood of the gutter, and dead cats floating in the water, helps us get a realistic picture of the shower.

2. The couplet works well to tie various images together in a forceful, realistic picture.

William Wordsworth

I WANDERED LONELY AS A CLOUD

1. Wordsworth puts together an iambic tetrameter quatrain and an imabic tetrameter couplet to form a six-line stanza.

2. The first three stanzas are a recounting of the perception of beauty. The last stanza concerns the recollection of beauty. This recollection, flashed on the "inward eye" when the speaker is in a pensive mood, is most important because it re-creates the moment of perception and makes eternal what has been at best fleeting and transitory.

Richard Hugo

2433 AGNES, FIRST HOME, LAST HOUSE IN MISSOULA

1. The sight of large numbers of buntings seem to impress the speaker of the poem in the same way that the daffodils inspire Wordsworth. The effect in the Hugo poem seems immediate, while the point of the Wordsworth poem is that much of the effect is not felt or known until later.

2. The speaker makes the first point by saying, "I believe/ no one should own land [because] You can't respect/ what you own."

Second, the poem says we must respect the land, not merely use it. Third, he points out that paying for something which cannot be bought depreciates our own value. Finally, the "trespassing" birds illustrate that property, or land, belongs to all inhabitants of the planet.

3. The birds take only what they need, and their presence in the ecosystem of Agnes Street and its environs indicates that they contribute to the life cycle. Their presence in the poem proves their contribution on other than biological levels.

Gerard Manley Hopkins

FELIX RANDAL

1. The poetic form is a Petrarchan or Italian sonnet. The emphasis in the first part, or octave, of the poem is on the spiritual aspects of the man Felix Randal and of his sickness and death. The second part, or sestet, of the sonnet deals with attractive aspects of the mortal man and of his vigor and life.

2. Effective sound devices Hopkins uses are end-rhyme, such as "handsome/ and some," lines 2 and 3; assonance, such as "great grey drayhorse," line 14; and alliteration, such as "My tongue had taught thee comfort, touch had quenched thy tears," line 10. They emphasize meaning by catching and holding our attention.

3. The last line of the poem is the most powerful, in terms of both thought and language. We get a vivid picture of the man, his work, and what he was made of as Felix Randal "Didst fettle for the great grey drayhorse his bright and battering sandal!"

Patricia Washington McGraw

BLUESBLACK

1. Lines 13 and 17 evoke especially powerful images. The first of these suggests the idea of blacks being sinister and predatory. The second calls for an almost opposite response when it prompts the reader to remember and to think about the squalor in which many poor blacks are forced to live.

2. The line is not trite for two reasons: it is a convention of the blues genre and as such is appropriate here; the line is poignant when we see it as a stark statement of frustration.

3. The line refers to the attitude of many in white society that blacks can and should be ignored, although ultimately their presence cannot be denied.

Elizabeth Jennings

ANSWERS

1. Stanzas one and two are regularly rhymed <u>axa</u>, <u>bxb</u>. After that
   the rhyme disappears. This breakdown in the rhyme scheme contributes to the theme of the poem in that change emulates the
   redirection of the speaker's thinking.

2. The small answers here may be termed the "local" ones, limited
   in time and space. They refer to the private circumstances of
   the speaker and ignore the possibility of placing the speaker's
   situation within a larger frame of reference. The large answers
   may be termed "universal" in that they address problems and
   questions faced by all members of the human race. By occupying
   oneself with the small answers, it may be possible to ignore—
   at least for a time—the relationships between one's own life
   and the rest of the world.

3. Shutting out the large answers seems short-sighted at best, and
   ultimately probably futile, especially in light of the poem's
   last line.

Joy Harjo

SOMEONE TALKING

1. The statement might refer to the power of language to make
   things happen. For example, words induced by reflections made
   in the course of the poem may help explain the speaker's
   situation to herself, thus inviting movement of some kind. Alternatively, unimportant or dangerous language can be shut out
   by moving one's attention elsewhere.

2. The speaker is Nonnie Daylight, an American Indian. The poem
   depicts the clash of opposites felt by Indian people: the sense
   of being an alien, suspect or patronized, in one's own land, and
   the old cultural conviction that the individual is firmly inte-
   grated and rooted in the cosmos.

3. Here we find the certainty of the speaker's conviction of her
   own firm place in the universe.

CHAPTER 13   ALLUSION AND SYMBOL

John Keats

ON FIRST LOOKING INTO CHAPMAN'S HOMER

1. Keats's mistaking Cortez for Balboa should be something the students would be willing to forgive the poet, since few of them probably know the distinction anyhow. The aim of this question is to stimulate discussion about historical allusions, which obviously should be factual enough to be recognized and understood. Still, the point should be made that the students have to recognize an allusion before they can attempt to understand it.

2. Keats conveys the measure of his excitement by a simile: "like some watcher of the skies/When a new planet swims into his ken." Since the simile itself carries the notion of wonderment and discovery, students who fail to see the importance of the Balboa/Cortez allusion should nevertheless be able to grasp the poem's central point.

William Butler Yeats

LONG-LEGGED FLY

1. Yeats is alluding to Michael Angelo's painting on the ceiling of the Sistine Chapel at the behest of Pope Julius II. The artist depicted scenes from providential history, and one of the most widely reproduced details of that work is God reaching out to imbue Adam with life. Thus, the allusion is both biblical and historical, and Yeats provides the reader with a double point of entry into the allusive quality of the stanza. By combining a mythical act with historical fact, Yeats goes on to underscore the inspirational source that is the mythical, whether it is classical or biblical. Heroic visions inspire subsequent heroic acts; the Creation inspires Michael Angelo's artistic reaction.

2. The insightful student should answer no to the first question. Yeats's choric simile—"Like a long-legged fly upon the stream/ His mind moves upon silence"—can easily be analyzed as a metaphor for the mind, or human psyche, moving upon the stream of

69

history or time. The latter becomes a reservoir supporting the former, but without the former there is not any human point of reference by which to measure that movement.

Andrew Marvell

TO HIS COY MISTRESS

1. Biblical allusions include those to Noah's flood, which ended the first covenant and led to the second, and to the conversion of the Jews, an act that providential history tells us will precede the final covenant, the Second Coming and Last Judgment. With those allusions, Marvell circumscribes all known time as the time of love. That the world and time he describes are reminiscent too of the Garden of Eden and a prelapsarian state might be noted; but the point should be well established that "ten years before the flood" clearly places the speaker in a fallen universe. As idyllic as the first stanza is, it still presents his coy mistress and the reader with a universe that is limited, not eternal.

2. Marvell's argument can easily be reduced to the following line of reasoning: If we had all the time in the world, I could forgive your coyness; but we do not have very much time before old age and death robbing us of our passions; therefore, you should stop being coy, and we should enjoy ourselves and our youth while we are able to. In purely logical terms, Marvell's conclusion is a valid inference from the major and minor premise; but it is not the only inference that can be drawn, nor is the issue at stake a purely logical matter.

3. Marvell's references to time and to the distances that can be placed between lovers both underscore the basic anxiety that his argument is founded on, that is, any lovers' fear of separation from each other. Marvell simply uses hyperbole--if the lovers had all of the world and all its time--to reinforce the fact that they really have a limited quantity of time and space to share with each other.

T. S. Eliot

THE LOVE SONG OF J. ALFRED PRUFROCK

1. There is the barest hint of an allusion to Marvell in lines 23-24 of the Eliot poem; i.e., the repetition of the refrain, "There will be time," which could be taken as a play on Marvell's first verse, "Had we but world enough, and time." However, that hint would remain a hint only were it not for the far more intentional and obvious allusion to Marvell in lines 87-98 of the Eliot poem. The direction of that stanza culminates in the image of squeezing "the universe into a ball/To roll it toward some overwhelming question," a clear play upon

Marvell's "Let us roll all our strength and all/Our sweetness up into one ball." That Eliot has Prufrock allude to the Marvell verses in the very stanza in which Prufrock's attempt at some resolution of the dilemma of time is frustrated, universalizes that frustration as well as the continuing attempts toward resolution. Neither Marvell's physical solution—give vent to passion and lust—nor Prufrock's metaphysical questings in a world of equally coy ladies should satisfy the careful reader; but each attempt underscores a peculiarly human dilemma dealt with in countless other poems, and Eliot's allusion to Marvell further underscores that fact.

2. The allusion to Lazarus is obviously a biblical allusion, although the identity and significance of Lazarus are both such commonplaces in our culture that some students may insist that the allusion is actually a symbol as that device is later defined in this chapter. In either case, Eliot's—and Prufrock's —use of Lazarus is mainly for shock effect. There is, indeed, something very comical in the fact that, even if Prufrock did come into a room declaring that he is Lazarus returned from the dead, he still does not feel that his presence would stir the others in that room. Thus, the allusion gives us insights into both Prufrock's self-image and his idea of the shallowness of the society he moves in.

3. Students should realize that Yeats's "Michael Angelo" and Eliot's "Michelangelo" are the same historical personage, i.e., the sixteenth-century Italian artist. The point to be made is that each poet is alluding to that historical figure for different purposes: Yeats to give us an image of the heroic; Eliot to give us a sense of the cultural snobbery of the women coming and going in Prufrock's world. In another sense, Yeats wants us to think of the artist himself, while Eliot wants us to picture the kind of people who would drop such an artist's name in among their small talk. Something, too, might be made of the fact that the women talk about Michelangelo, but Prufrock is sure they would hardly notice him even if he were Lazarus.

Epigraph. The epigraph from Dante provides its own ironies and sets the stage for ironies within the poem. Da Montefeltro speaks freely only because he is sure that his interlocutor is a condemned soul like himself. Obviously, that is not the case, and Dante will return to tell the tale of da Montefeltro's infamy. In the same way, we could argue that Prufrock is speaking from his own hell to a person or persons (whether it is simply himself is beside the point) who share that hell with him. Thus, he too speaks freely; we should not feel that he is concealing anything. Furthermore, we could argue that the joke is finally on the reader; Eliot could be setting up Prufrock as a mirror of ourselves and our ability to empathize. Finally, then, both in Dante's verses and in Eliot's use of them, there is the suggestion that genuine human communication depends upon empathy with and from kindred souls and that that essential human quality survives death itself.

POETRY

Sylvia Plath

DADDY

1. "Dachau, Auschwitz, Belsen" is a historical allusion to the
   atrocities of Nazi genocide. Further allusions to those historical events, i.e., the Nazis, the extermination of the Jews,
   and World War II in general, could be said to be contained in
   every reference to Germany, Germans, Polish (Polack), Jews,
   Vienna, Tyrol, etc. Some of the more obscure of such allusions
   are possibly found in Luftwaffe (the Nazi air force), Aryan
   (Hitler's name for his master race), Panzer (the Nazi tank
   force), swastika (the Nazi symbol), and Mein Kampf (Hitler's
   pseudo-philosophical and racist autobiography). Plath, by
   weaving such allusions and their significances into a poem ostensibly addressed to her father, establishes a connection between the tyrannies and terrors of political fascism and the
   age-old conflicts between father and daughter, parent and child,
   over hard-fisted parental authority. The poem could be summed
   up in the paraphrase "Fascism begins at home."

2. Plath's references to a "vampire" and "a stake in your fat black
   heart" are obvious allusions to so-called horror films dealing
   with Dracula. Not only were such films popular in America in
   the thirties, the decade preceding the war, but the vogue began
   with the German Expressionist film movement during the twenties,
   the decade during which Hitler wrote Mein Kampf and which ended
   with the economic collapse of the Weimar Republic, thus paving
   the way for the Nazis' taking power in Germany in the early
   thirties. Beyond those connections, any notion of vampirism—
   one person using another for his or her own pleasures—comments
   strongly once more on the way in which Plath views her relationship with her father: he would take her very life-blood if he
   could, while she, Elektra-fashion, would like to wipe him out
   in the best style of vampire-killing. Pit this popular version/
   vision of horror and terror and murder against the other allusions to Nazi atrocities in the poem, and the result is an un-
   avoidable connection between all that is wrong with society—its
   values, its tastes, its brutalities, its flagrant acts of in-
   humanity, its violence—and all that is wrong with the family
   structure. The poem becomes an indictment not only of the
   speaker's father, but of the popular culture that spawns, at the
   same time, their destructive relationship and the mass destruc-
   tiveness of the Nazis.

Imamu Amiri Baraka (LeRoi Jones)

IN MEMORY OF RADIO

1. Because of the endless waves of pop culture, high camp, and
   nostalgia crazes, your students may recognize quite a few of
   the celebrities, actual and fictional, alluded to in Baraka's
   poem. Kate Smith, always thirty pounds lighter, is always making a comeback. Jack Kerouac, now dead, may be forgotten, since
   the Beat Generation is now dead too and Kerouac turned

72

conservative in his later years. Oral Roberts not only does TV
revivals regularly, but has a university in Oklahoma named after
him. F[ulton] J. Sheen, besides officiating at Midnight Mass
every other Christmas from St. Patrick's, has a weekly show on
PBS. Lamont Cranston as the Shadow may have, by now, assumed
mythical proportions among the with-it and cognoscenti, and the
same probably holds true for Mandrake. I don't know who Goody
Knight was—or is—and am not very familiar with Red Lantern and
Let's Pretend, except to say that they were obviously old radio
programs. Hitler, meanwhile, needs no introduction. It is
probably sufficient to say, as pop journalists would, that the
interplay of these various figures "recaptures an era." Beyond
that, however, the fact that so many of the figures are either
connected with unregenerate chauvinism (Kate Smith, Hitler) or
spoon-fed religious buckupsterism (Sheen, Roberts) or simplistic
notions of good vs. evil (the Shadow, Mandrake) suggests levels
of meaning to the poem that your students may want to probe.

2. For the above-stated reasons, your students may have found Baraka's allusions nearly as obscure as, say, Yeats's or Keats's, and
certainly Eliot's. Baraka's awareness of this possible dated-
ness of campy allusions is implied in the very fact that he
wrote the poem, thus keeping the "memory of radio" alive a little longer.

Michael S. Harper

LOVE MEDLEY: PATRICE CUCHULAIN

1. Harper is suggesting many things with the child's name, but he
is basically suggesting that, as a black in America, the child
will need to have a strong sense of his personal identity in
order to survive and that he can obtain the strongest sense of
himself as a man and as a human being by being identified in
name with heroes of other peoples who have also been oppressed,
i.e., African colonial subjects and the Irish.

2. The child "weighs in" like a prize fighter, and he is six feet
and thirteen inches long, as clear an instance of a proud father's engaging in hyperbole as can be found in literature.

3. The poem tells us that the child had two older brothers who
died at birth. Furthermore, the precise detail with which the
birth process is described emphasizes the wonder and respect
with which the speaker approaches the action.

Alta

THE VOW

1. For the poet, Anne Hutchinson is doubly heroic, once for the
actual blow she struck for religious freedom, and then once

more for having done so even though she was a woman in a man's
world. The fact of Hutchinson's obscurity proves to the poet's
satisfaction how much women have been relegated to historical
footnotes, no matter what their accomplishments. Finally, however, the poet realizes that the current spirit of feminism will
bring Hutchinson and others like her, whom the history books
have slighted, back to life as role models and heroic figures
for young women.

2. The poet vows that no woman will ever again suffer the fate of
being ignored or forgotten for accomplishments which, if a man
had achieved them, would have assured recognition and respect,
and she makes that vow not only to Hutchinson but to her own
female forebears as well. Thus, for the poet, Hutchinson becomes a feminist heroine more than a mere advocate of religious
tolerance.

3. The pun is on the traditional role of women as homemakers; in
that sense, Hutchinson's name is not a household word because
she was not content to do nothing more than keep house. The
same statement is also an allusion to Spiro Agnew's similar and
famous remark about himself in his acceptance speech for the
Republican vice-presidential nomination in 1968. Alta no doubt
finds it ironic that a figure such as Anne Hutchinson is forgotten because she was a woman while a man such as Spiro Agnew
can become vice president and then go on to disgrace the office
by taking bribes.

Robert Frost

DESIGN

1. Frost reverses the usual logic of the sonnet in this poem. Instead of asking the questions in the octet and answering them
in the sestet, he questions the octet in the sestet. Largely
what he is questioning is the imagination's own ability, through
its propensity for finding likenesses and symbols in the natural
world, to force itself up against the wall of its own terrors.
Read symbolically, the natural objects in the first stanza certainly become threatening images of a universal intelligence
with a macabre sense of humor. But the entire poem is posited
on a conditional that is not stated till the very end: "If
design govern in a thing so small." That condition is the point
the entire poem leads us toward. Was this confluence of spider,
moth, flower, and poet another sort of ruling intelligence? No
doubt Frost wants to tease us into thinking, but necessarily into meaning. If your students say, "Yes, design does govern in
a thing so small," then ask them to discuss what it might all
mean. If they say that it doesn't, then ask them at what point
design does start governing and why. Either way, the poem will
be serving the function for which Frost designed it: to arouse
our sensibilities by forcing us to regard the smallest things
in the most serious ways.

2. Through similes, Frost likens the dead moth to a <u>white piece of rigid satin cloth</u>, the <u>characters of death and blight</u> to <u>the ingredients of a witches' broth</u>, and the moth's wings to <u>a paper kite</u>. Whatever each of these images may finally be analyzed as signifying, the relationships which Frost establishes as well keep the reader within a particular sphere of reference. Not only does that sphere of reference force the reader to see the spider, moth and flower as meaning something more than simply a spider, moth, and flower, but the associations force the reader to see something unquestionably peculiar and possibly threatening and terrifying in the otherwise accidental <u>design</u>. Why a <u>white piece of rigid satin cloth</u>, which suggests the consecration of the Eucharist? Why a <u>witches' broth</u>, which more than suggests black magic? What is being brewed—consecrated—in that figurative chalice? And then, the almost ludicrous and certainly downbeat notion of an innocent <u>paper kite</u> is introduced. Is Frost implying that even the terrifying is blessed, or that the blessed is also terrifying when all the connections are made?

3. Frost does not present us with traditional oppositions in "Design." Indeed, the whiteness of the flower, moth, and spider is every bit as disconcerting, in Frost's view, as darkness, as if to suggest that too much of anything is not good. In the final analysis, then, the plethora of whiteness in the poem has the same effect on our psyches, and on the speaker's, as the whiteness of the whale in <u>Moby Dick</u>.

Miller Williams

BELIEVING IN SYMBOLS

1. When Williams says that symbols have led us into war and into bed with interesting people, he is reminding us of the blurred distinctions between object or concept and the symbol of that object or concept. Certainly the swastika seems more than just a symbol and, under the proper circumstances, could lead us into war again. In the same way, designer jeans may look no better and no worse than a run-of-the-mill item but do make a variety of symbolic statements about the value system of the wearer. As a race, we are still capable of defending a flag which, its symbolic value aside, is nevertheless nothing more than a piece of cloth; and it was only after actress Loni Anderson switched from being a brunette to being a blond that she become not only a star but a sexy one at that.

2. Williams is making a literal statement when he says that 8 has become the "figure all figures are made from" with solid state electronics, as anyone who has ever seen a digital display board knows. He uses that fact, however, to comment on how everything passes, and he certainly feels that that transience is applicable to other things--the pterodactyl, the Packard, Pompeii—besides symbols.

3. Williams uses the metaphor of the coin to show how the symbol
   and the thing symbolized are simply two sides of the same reality, the one which we create with our words and symbols and the
   one which is objectively itself. Still, it is the symbolic significance which we attach to an object—the name of a planet,
   for example—that is important to us and that, in the long run,
   becomes the object of our attention. Without our symbols, then,
   we would have little way of identifying and thus of distinguishing, and the universe would lose its human face and become a
   cold, abstract, objective reality with no place for us in it.

Judith Moffett

BIOLOGY LESSON

1. The "buccal groove" is a mouth, essentially, and the actions of
   paramecia as they reproduce thus become connotative of aspects
   of human lovemaking, particularly kissing.

2. The word schism certainly has a literal meaning, but we are encouraged to hear the poet playing with the figurative concepts
   the word arouses, particularly the emotional pains of depletion
   and separation which often follow intense lovemaking. The point
   is not, of course, whether or not the paramecia feel such pain
   but that in their action we see a symbolic rendering of our own
   actions. Thus the word schism is a symbol of the gulf that
   separates humans—loving creatures who are nevertheless separate
   and distinct individual entities before and after any sexual
   union. The third stanza emphasizes the link between the poet's
   subject and human love.

3. Moffett is having the same fun as Benchley did with his parody.
   She parodies a biology lesson where we learn about the biological processes of paramecia but seldom are taught about our own
   sexual functionings. At the heart of Moffett's sentiment about
   the "paramecium's sex life" is not wit and literary mockery so
   much as a deep and abiding respect for the delicacies and ex-
   quisite beauties of natural processes, particularly those associated with reproduction.

Edmund Spenser

SONNET 81

1. The rose in her cheeks can be seen as symbolizing health, youth,
   and beauty, as well as a certain measure of sexual passion. The
   subsequent line—"in her eyes the fyre of love does sparke"—
   lends credence to the latter connotation. Surely the rose
   is intended as something more than a mere description of hue,
   and your students should recognize as much.

2. The final detail that Spenser selects to describe his beloved—
and to gain our attention—is the intelligence and gentleness
of her speech; for Spenser, beauty is more than skin deep.
Further, the last two lines dismiss the physical beauties in
favor of spiritual ones. In that sense, the rose could be seen
as an 'emblem of the beloved's purity.

William Shakespeare

SONNET 130

1. Some of your students may see Shakespeare's omission of roses
from his mistress's cheeks as honesty on his part; others may
see him as being insulting to her or witty at her expense.
Whatever their various reactions, all should agree that Shakespeare depends for his poem's effect on our being familiar
with the syrupy elegance of descriptions found in love sonnets
such as Spenser's "Sonnet 81."

2. Shakespeare succeeds by setting us up, of course. By line 12
he has so demeaned and ridiculed his mistress's beauty, apparently, that few first readers are ready for the poignantly
telling turn of the couplet. Once a student discerns the bard's
strategy, which is to eschew a literary style for the sake of
a literal praise, most forgive Shakespeare at the expense of
poets such as Spenser.

3. Naturally, Shakespeare engages as much in hyperbole as Spenser
and his school do; because Shakespeare plays the role of the
literary iconoclast, however, he is more likely to gain the
respect of beginning students. His mockery of the genre is
clear from such figures of speech as black wires (4) and breath
that reeks (8).

William Blake

THE SICK ROSE

1. Blake's rose can be seen as representing all good things:
youthful beauty, innocence, young love—whatever is finally
not only transient but fragile and vulnerable. The "invisible
worm" thus becomes not so much death as the seed of corruption
that inevitably invades all that is substantial and beautiful
and innocent. The shock effect of Blake's poem, like Shakespeare's "Sonnet 130," is founded on a readership that is used
to encountering roses as emblematic of physical and spiritual
health and wholesomeness rather than real roses, which are
susceptible to corruption and decay.

Paul Laurence Dunbar

PROMISE

1. There is nothing in the Dunbar poem to suggest that he is not talking about a literal rose in a literal garden. The perceptive student will see this poem as a fine illustration of how symbol-hunting can cause readers to lose sight of equally valuable surface beauties and lessons based on literal experiences.

2. Students who wish to read Dunbar's poem as an exercise in symbolic statement will no doubt come up with a wide variety of interpretations. Generally, they will be on the right track if they view the rose as something of precious value to the speaker, a thing which he has had to nurture, and the thoughtless child as representative of indifference and carelessness. The poem offers a decidedly valuable lesson in the conflicts between individual hopes and aspirations, on the one hand, and the vicissitudes of the great world, on the other. Emphasize, nevertheless, that that lesson is rendered as well on the literal level as on any symbolic level in this poem.

John Crowe Ranson

PIAZZA PIECE

1. A dustcoat was an item of outer wear worn in earlier days to protect travelers' clothing from the dirt and grime of long-distance journeys, and it survived into the early days of automotive travel. While it has a definite literal meaning, students should see how the notion of an aged coachman or driver, as well as the implications of dust itself, is connotative of death. Ransom maintains the literal level throughout the poem, but we can assume that he wants us to see the "gentleman in a dustcoat," "an old man," a "gray man," as symbolic of the coming of old age, if not of death.

2. Ransom's gentleman apparently is schooled in poetic tradition. His reference to the roses dying on her trellis is his way of providing her with a gentle—and natural—memento mori. Since the young lady clearly wants to hear nothing about topics such as decay and death, the gentleman's task is all that much more necessary, if difficult.

William Carlos Williams

THE ROSE

1. Your students should quickly pick up William's assertion as a reference to the rose's vitality as a symbol rather than its currency as a flower. A flower cannot become obsolete, but by overuse a flower's symbolic significances can very easily

become tired, and hence obsolete. (Remind students that obsolescence relates to a thing's usefulness, not its state of delapidation.

2. A flower's petals do indeed penetrate space, just as surely as a blade of steel might. A flower's petal can also figuratively penetrate the spaces within our minds precisely because poets such as Williams can "plant" symbolic flowers there.

Marcela Christine Lucero

ROSEVILLE, MINN., U.S.A.

1. Lucero makes Roseville into an archetypal American white middle-class enclave, a place where life—and all its appurtenances—are "rosy," and very pleasantly so. Thus the town becomes a symbol of spick-and-span, white-enriched-bread American values, the homogenized product of mainstream North American culture, for which the speaker's values and customs are either quaint or outré. Lucero's theme, of course, is that from the point of view of her Mexican-American background, it is the Anglo customs and values that are strange.

2. Your students will probably conclude that Lucero makes rosy and rose seem like dirty words, connotative of blandness, cultural shortsightedness, and shallow value systems. Indeed, while Lucero's criticism of the white America that Roseville represents is more gently poking fun than vitriolic, there are very few positive connotations for rose and rosy in the poem.

3. She speaks of it as a foreign culture, a place where people of Mexican descent are either mistaken for Spaniards or mistaken for migrant workers, where her diet is "un-American," and where she feels constantly that she is being asked to sell out or conceal her own people's traditions. In Roseville, one fits in or disappears behind drawn drapes and shut windows. While Lucero's tone is neither bitter nor envious, it is also not very matter-of-fact, and your better students will use words such as ironic, sarcastic, and satirical.

CHAPTER 14   THE SCHEME OF MEANING

John Donne

HYMN TO GOD MY GOD, IN MY SICKNESS

1. Just as a map—or planisphere—can represent the earth, which is
   actually spherical, by making the furthest western point match
   the furthest eastern point, so "death doth touch the resurrection" both by harking back to the promise of eternal life given
   in Christ's resurrection and by the resurrection of each soul,
   upon the body's death, into its eternal life. If the statement
   does contain a paradox, it is simply because Donne's belief in
   an eternal life after death is a central tenet of _faith_ in
   Christianity. From a Christian point of view, then, there is
   no paradox at all. Indeed, one cannot have a resurrection unless there is a death.

2. Obviously, the Pacific Sea _is_ the Pacific Sea (or Ocean), which
   one would find to the western side of a map. Still, if one goes
   east, of course, one will also find the Pacific. Finally, there
   is the clear pun on _pacific_, both the proper noun denoting a
   specific ocean and an adjective suggesting the peace of death,
   the soul's final resting place.

3. _He_ can refer back to Christ and to Adam. But because it can
   also refer to the mortal individual now dying and be a reference forward to _the Lord_, the final verse points many ways.
   Donne sees himself embodying both the first Adam (father of fall-
   en mankind) and the last—or second—Adam (Christ, the perfect
   man) as his savior. Thus, a number of Christian paradoxes can
   be read into that final verse: the _felix culpa_ (Adam's fall at
   least left mankind with the joys of experiencing salvation);
   Adam's fall led to the miracle of Christ's birth, death, and
   resurrection; one must die (be _throw[n] down_ bodily) to be born
   again (to _r[a]ise_); in the scheme of the trinity, the Lord as
   God the creator gives life and takes it away, and Christ through
   his sacrifice allows the means for that mortal life to gain
   eternal life ("that he [Christ] may raise [us to heaven] the
   Lord throws down [gives us life and death]").

4. We would immediately have to say "in Christ's purple wrapped,"
   as statuary is wrapped in purple during Lent. Perhaps wrapped
   in Christ's blood too; i.e., _wrapped_ as _embraced_. But because
   of the earlier question about the proper reference of _he_, some

80

of your students may want to argue that <u>his</u> refers back to Adam as well, since Adam's blood is Donne's heritage—from which the blood of Christ shall save him.

George Herbert

VIRTUE

1. Dew, like <u>tear</u>-like droplets, does indeed come after night<u>fall</u>.

2. The pattern is logical and cumulative: day is addressed and told that it shall die, the dew weeping its <u>fall</u>; the rose is addressed, followed by a reference to tears, and then told that it shall die, with a paradoxical comment on how its life-giving roots are grounded in the very earth that shall be the rose's grave; <u>sweet spring</u>, <u>compacted</u> of <u>sweet day</u> and <u>sweet roses</u>, the respective subject of each earlier stanza, is told that it too must die. Only a "sweet <u>and virtuous</u> soul," which is compared, in contrast with the passing day and fragile rose, with "seasoned timber," will not die. <u>The seasoned timber</u>, reminding us of trees purposively removed from the cycles of nature, is finally further connected with <u>coal</u>, a substance that seasoned timber would become should it be burned. But even then, Herbert says—especially then—the soul <u>chiefly lives</u>. Thus, Herbert carries us through cyclical nature as a <u>memento mori</u> that the soul transcends and finally overcomes. The beauty of this poem is that the movement is carried as much through the interlinking imagery as through the meaning religiously considered. From nature to something wrested from nature to something transcending nature: the soul. Consequently, the <u>lie</u> compacted in <u>a</u> <u>box</u>—also a thing made of wood—is the lie that nature tells us: all things are born, change, and die. The virtuous soul, superceding those natural processes, does not die, though it can be compared to things in nature for the purposes of poetry.

3. This question has been largely answered in the preceding treatment. I do think that it is difficult to resist the logic of Herbert's resolution—that for the soul to live, the world must die—simply because the message is established poetically first, intellectually second. Long before the reader realizes what Herbert is leading toward, his images have carried us to his conclusion. Indeed, the function of the imagery is to make us see the possible truth in a logical pattern as smooth as an extended syllogism. That such a logic is only implied is further proof of the poem <u>qua</u> poetry.

Ben Jonson

A HYMN TO GOD THE FATHER

1. Jonson's paradox in the first stanza is very similar to the one in Donne's final verse above: our suffering is our salvation, since it leads us to eschew the things of this world.

81

2. The allusion is to the Roman soldiers who threw dice for Christ's robe beneath the cross of his crucifixion. Jonson twists it, so that to lose at the earthly—and, by allusion, blasphemous—game of chance is to win at a game whose stakes are higher, being his eternal soul. The poem in a sense paraphrases the biblical admonition: "For what shall it profit a man if he gain the whole world and lose his immortal soul?" Obviously, there is a rich texture of religious punning and paradox to the poem, making it worth further discussion.

Daniela Gioseffi

WHEAT

1. Students should be encouraged to recognize that maggots and sperm are similar not only because they are both related to reproductive processes but also because they are similar in shape and color. Maggots also have the same general configurations as kernels of wheat, and both are part of the food chain. Gioseffi is trying to force us to see an interconnectedness and systemic beauty among and in all things; if her suggestions offend some of your students, encourage them to think about the objects and processes that she is describing in the way that a research scientist would think about them.

2. There should be no question that Gioseffi experiences an intellectual pleasure, and perhaps a spiritual pleasure as well, in the similarities she has discovered among apparently disparate objects: maggots, sperm, and wheat. The concluding exclamation mark alone is sufficient proof that she has been surprised by joy, so to speak. This might provide an appropriate juncture to remind your students of the metaphorical validity of observation on which almost all poetry, and certainly all figurative uses of language, is founded.

William Blake

HOLY THURSDAY [I] HOLY THURSDAY [II]

1. If the students accept [II] as expressing Blake's true feelings—and they may simply because the second of the pair is so much bitterer and angrier in tone—they should begin to question his sincerity in [I]. It would help to tell them that beadles were not kindly old men but protofascists charged with keeping a brutal authority in force, and that their snow-white wands are very likely caning sticks, etc. Obviously, a reader needs not only the context of [II] but a sense of the social context of the times to enjoy [I] more fully. Some experience of Dickens, particularly Oliver Twist, might help.

2. Because the poem asks questions, albeit rhetorical ones, your students may be unsure that their answers are the ones Blake

wishes to elicit. The final stanza should assist them. Babes
do hunger and poverty does appall everywhere on earth and
throughout history, yet so has the sun shone and rain fallen.
Blake, then, is either stupid for thinking that one set of phen-
omena should preclude the other or, once more, bitter and cynical. Once readers find themselves in such a dilemma, they
should give the benefit of the doubt to the author. If the man
can write a poem, he can't be that stupid. Therefore he is
being bitter and cynical—which is the very direction in which
the earlier rhetorical questions ought to have led the reader.
The poem is a brain-teaser of sorts. If the first three are
false, the last is true. Because any human being ought to know
that the last stanza is a false assessment of the state of the
world, the first three stanzas are true.

Percy Bysshe Shelley

OZYMANDIAS

1. Perceptive students will see that the poem is constructed like
   boxes within boxes: the first speaker tells us what the traveler told him, and that information includes the words of Ozymandias. The traveler's closing observation suggests that he is
   aware of the irony which Ozymandias's words convey in their
   present context of utter desolation. Whether or not all agree
   that the traveler senses that irony, students should see that,
   ironically, Ozymandias's words now mock rather than accentuate
   his glory and power.

2. We can easily assume that Ozymandias meant the words to strike
   fear and trembling into the reader's heart, whose despair would
   come from realizing how mighty is the state of Ozymandias. The
   traveler no doubt feels that the words should continue to strike
   fear and trembling into our hearts, not because of Ozymandias's
   power, but because there is nothing left.

3. The sculptor surely read Ozymandias's vainglorious personality
   and, if that sculptor was any student of philosophy, no doubt
   knew that Ozymandias's boast would someday come back to mock
   him. While there is the suggestion here that art survives
   power, we should also realize that the same desert winds that
   have reduced the rest of Ozymandias's kingdom to rubble will one
   day reduce these remnants of the sculptor's statue to rubble.
   Thus, the paradox of the poem is that even artistic efforts cannot overcome the eventual decay wrought by the passage of time,
   though for the moment we feel that it is the sculptor and not
   Ozymandias who was triumphant and who created something enduring. The poem clearly says that nothing is enduring; some
   things just last longer than others; e.g., artistic creations
   last longer than political and military prowess.

Robert Browning

MY LAST DUCHESS

1. Students may be divided on the veracity of the Duke's insistence
   that he is interested only in the Count's daughter rather than
   in her dowry, but most will be inclined to imagine that the
   Duke is an out-and-out materialist. As for object, more perceptive students will see at least an ambiguity: object as goal
   or aim; object as a thing to be possessed. No one can say
   whether the Duke is himself aware of the ambiguity, and of its
   resulting irony, but the question should provide for a few minutes of heated debate on Browning's technique.

2. The Duke's constant use of the first-person singular pronoun
   is the most immediate and obvious indicator of his overweening
   and overbearing sense of self. His insistence that only he
   should draw back the curtain covering his last duchess's portrait, his bragging about his nine-hundred-years-old name, and
   his outrage over the duchess's inability to dote solely on him
   should all be called up as evidence of the Duke's arrogance and
   self-importance. Finally, his solution to the dilemma that the
   duchess's openness and friendliness created for him can leave no
   one in doubt as to the Duke's jealousy and possessiveness.
   While it is very likely that the Duke is not aware of the negative impression his words might be making, students should see
   that, if he were apprised of it, he probably would not care—
   and that a measure of his arrogance is calculated to impress the
   Count through his emissary.

3. Most students will agree that the duchess was put to death, at
   worst, or put into a dungeon or convent. Certainly no one will
   dispute that she was put aside with dispatch and very likely
   without mercy.

4. The significance of that closing reference to the Neptune "cast
   in bronze for me" is manifold. For one thing, the poem ends
   with the first-person singular pronoun. For another, the remark
   reveals, far more than pride of ownership, an almost pathologi-
   cal possessiveness. Furthermore, the Duke makes little distinction between a human life—his last duchess—and his other
   possessions; they are valuable only inasmuch as they are his
   and his alone. When the duchess ceased to be only his, she
   ceased as well to be of value to him. Now, however, he has
   her forever among his collection of objets d'art, on a plane
   with all his other valuable possessions.

Ishmael Reed

BEWARE : DO NOT READ THIS POEM

1. Reed no doubt wishes to entice readers into his poem, in much
   the same way as the old woman in the mirror entices unwary

tenants into the mirror. Thus, the chatty, street-wise tone is fully intended.

2. The poem is partly a discourse on the spellbinding qualities of art, particularly storytelling. It is also a commentary on the moral obligations of art: the artist in a very real sense does take us over to suit his or her purposes. In the poem, then, we see ourselves for the paradoxical creatures we are, willing to be scared out of our wits by a horror movie or by a poem but very likely unaware of real horrors such as the annual disappearance of 100,000 people in America alone. The poem ultimately reflects on how we generally regard real tragedies as dull and dry when they do not affect us, and yet easily become totally embroiled in fictions—the more tragically horrible the better.

3. Reed's conclusion of the poem with the statistic on missing persons is his way of saying that fact is stranger—and more disconcerting—than fiction. Too, the statistic reinforces the poem's implied theme: tell a tale of horror and everyone will listen raptly; impart an awful fact and people will listen politely and then go on to something else. Thus we are allowed to see the irony that our fictions, no matter how horrific, protect us from something that is potentially more horrible, i.e., life itself.

Thomas Hardy

AH, ARE YOU DIGGING ON MY GRAVE?

1. Though the words of the third speaker are simply being reported by the speaker, they are represented as a direct quotation. Thus, there are three speakers in the first stanza: the deceased, the dog, and the deceased's former love. A fourth speaker, the deceased's dearest kin, is similarly introduced into the second stanza. In both cases, the deceased's anticipation of who is digging and why is undercut by the dog's response. The same development occurs in the third stanza, wherein the deceased thinks that it might be her worst enemy. Again, the dog deflates even that expectation, but this time only reports the thoughts of that third party. Thus, there are four speakers in the poem: the two interlocutors, and the two reported statements.

2. Quite simply, the premise is that if such a conversation could ever take place, this is very likely how it might run. But the reader is so intent on discovering the identity of the digger, the patent absurdity of the situation slips by unnoticed. That the digger is the deceased's dog and that the dog is hardly there out of grief continue to keep us willingly suspending our disbelief until we reach the conclusion. By then, it should make little matter whether or not the conversation could ever take place; for all the surprise, wit, and humor of the poem, we are left with a sad truth that might have been mawkish if

presented otherwise: once a person dies, he or she is gradually
forgotten, not only by those who loved him, but by those who
hated him.   The beauty of the poem is not in its message, which
is debatably commonplace, but in Hardy's clever treatment of a
potentially maudlin subject.

e. e. cummings

NEXT TO OF COURSE GOD AMERICA I

1. Cummings is parodying the Sunday orator and Fourth of July en-
   comiast; in other words, any jingoistic spouter of public pap
   and patriotic pieties, particularly those of a politician.
   Since Cummings literally has the speaker running off at the
   mouth, we can assume that Cummings wants the speaker to sound
   like a thoughtless idiot, a recording device saying what it is
   supposed to.   That the speaker is presented as being mindless
   suggests that it would never occur to the speaker that he might
   sound ridiculous.   The final line of the poem tells us, for one
   thing, that the speaker is so busy voicing his nonsense he has
   failed to notice his own thirst.   Thus, the last line further
   enhances the image of the speaker as an empty-headed fool.   Too,
   it seems to be hardly punishment enough that his mouth should
   be dry only after such a tirade of inanities.

2. While Cummings toyed with punctuation sometimes for the mere
   sake of cuteness, in this poem the lack of punctuation is inte-
   gral to the impression we get of the speaker.   Such a lack suggests that he does not know—or care—where one thought ends and
   the other begins.   All he wants to do is to get it all out before he needs to quench his thirst—and perhaps without taking
   a breather either.   The tumble of words—most of them mottoes
   and catch-phrases—comes at us as rapidly and incoherently as
   they fall out of the speaker's mouth.   If they didn't, we would
   discover that he is talking nonsense, and dangerous nonsense to
   boot, because men die to the ring of such tunes.   That is what
   Cummings wants us to realize, and he achieves that goal by
   freezing such a speech on the page.

Gwendolyn Brooks

WE REAL COOL

1. The pool players very likely believe that they are real cool;
   there can be no question that Brooks does not share their opinion.   Most students will see this and will base their conclusion on the absurdist irony of the closing three words of the
   pool players' refrain.

2. Students will understand that the constant repetition of we illustrates that the pool players think only of themselves as a

group; they depend upon their identification as a group for meaning.

3. Clearly Brooks's poem achieves its effectiveness by sounding like the pool players and thus parodying their value system. If Brooks had spoken about them instead, she might have put some readers off—particularly those readers most in need of hearing her—by seeming to moralize or preach.

Naomi Lazard

MISSING FATHER REPORT

1. The poem sounds like a public notice advertisement, although some students might identify it as sounding like a wanted poster. The title, of course, also suggests that it is a report made to the police. Students should be encouraged to notice that the tone is that of a written rather than a spoken communication. Likely sources for such a report would include newspapers, magazines, and public bulletin boards.

2. We are forced to assume that it is the speaker's father who is missing, but he is not really missing so much as no longer an active, nurturing agent in the speaker's emotional life. Whatever may actually have become of the father, students should recognize that he has "checked out" on any involvement in the speaker's life.

3. Generally, the lead-in sentence to each stanza is written in a bureaucratic tone, while the remainder of the stanza drifts into a tone either of wry irony or of wistful longing. In the case of the fourth stanza, the bureaucratic tone disappears entirely. The speaker is ambivalent in feelings both toward her father and toward the fact that he has apparently abandoned her, and her emotional ambivalence is reflected in the varying and sudden shifts in tone and style as well as in the ironic context—a "missing father report"--in which her disappointment is expressed.

Ian Young

POEM FOUND IN A DIME-STORE DIARY

1. It should make no difference to the average reader if he or she discovers that Young actually made up the poem and was only pretending to have come across it by accident. It is a reasonable enough facsimile of the sorts of memory aids that calendar- and diary-printing companies provide to their customers for us to believe that Young did indeed come across it; but if he invented it, it still rings true. Partly its point is that poetry can be found in the most unlikely places and that "found"

poetry can make the sort of statement we have come to expect from highly conscious, crafted poetry.

2. The poem comments on the degrees and extent of our individual obligations to all the other people who have an active interest in our lives and general welfare, and it emphasizes how much each of us lives for tomorrow, perhaps at the expense of the here and now. By placing the "tomorrow is . . ." slips last, Young allows us to see how, if we continually live for tomorrow, our obligations will very likely never be satisfied and will merely continue to haunt us like a broken record. Again, Young has arranged the slips in such a way as to lead us to that conclusion, but does not state it outright.

W. H. Auden

MUSÉE DES BEAUX ARTS

1. The entire poem is constructed around a direct allusion to Pieter Brueghel's painting The Fall of Icarus, which hangs in the Museum of Fine Arts in Brussels. There is also the allusion to the Old Masters, other painters in the Flemish school, including notably Rembrandt and Vandyke. In the first stanza, there is an allusion to the Nativity and to another of Brueghel's paintings, picturing the Nativity as a central detail in a scene where children are skating in the background, etc. Finally, the last four lines are allusions to details from the painting The Martyrdom of St. Stephen. This interplay of open allusion, concealed allusion, and punning—e.g., the "miraculous birth" the aged await can be both the Nativity and each one's own death—forces the reader to see the human position of suffering through the eyes of artists, both the Old Masters and W. H. Auden. What the reader should see is that the busy world does not stop, nor should the sufferer necessarily expect it to do so.

2. It has been my experience that students immediately want to read this poem as a highly serious comment on—if not indictment of—human apathy. Once the student becomes aware that the highly conversational if not blasé tone (walking dully along; not specially want it to happen; untidy spot; doggy life; innocent behind) checks the tendency toward high seriousness in other phrases (reverently, passionately waiting; the dreadful martyrdom), he or she should be ready to give Auden his due. Auden is contrasting the facts of life—people are born, people die; some people, like Icarus, do stupid things, however heroic that stupidity may seem; some people suffer, but all mankind cannot stop to suffer with them—with the way we talk about such things, i.e., in high-faluting language and reverential whispers.

3. By now, your students should be willing to grant the possibility that Auden might really feel it to be quite proper that "everything turns away/Quite leisurely from the disaster." Should

the ploughman, laboring in his own drudgery, regard the fall of Icarus as an **important failure**? Should the sailing ship, pursuing a more pedestrian course than the adventuresome Icarus but still having **someplace to get to** of its own, have done anything more than **sailed calmly on**? Why should our sympathies go to Icarus and not to the poor ploughman, who is far from his own blessed release? Why should we feel sorry for Icarus's failing to complete his journey, if we want the sailing ship to stop its? Whatever your students may say in response to these questions, they are the questions the poem forces us to ask, and the opening verses tell us that such is the human position of suffering. No matter how much we, under the bane of our pieties, may insist we would have done something to help Icarus, if we had been there, we too would have gone on with our own necessary tasks.

Johari Amini

IDENTITY

1. The lefthand column is the speaker's report of the action, the right the conversation that the speaker and the poet engage in. Very likely students have an easier time following the flow of the poem if the lines had been arranged in a more traditional fashion, but that would have been contrary to the very purpose of the poem, which is a search for identity and for personal integration. The split effect which the poet thus achieves reflects the split in the speaker's own sense of herself, a split which has been healed by poem's end by the words of the poet.

2. Naturally, the two conclusions do jibe. Black pride is the speaker's identity, but what the poem illustrates is that she cannot have that identity until she is proud of being black.

3. Malcolm X was an early leader of the Black Muslim movement; W. E. B. DuBois was an educator and sociologist and a founder of the NAACP; James Baldwin and LeRoi Jones are two prominent contemporary black authors; Patrice Lumumba was a martyred exponent of black African nationalism; and Stokely Carmichael was an extremely articulate spokesman for black militancy in America during the late 1960s. In a poem dealing with black pride and the formulation of a black identity in America, each of those individuals, as well as the further references to the principles of the Black Muslim movement and black nationalism, underscore the poet's argument with the speaker: that she must think black if she is to be black and proud. Each individual named was to one degree or another an exponent of that same basic argument.

4. The speaker's language is a mixture of neutral American and black street talk ("a crown of natural"; "curlfree do"), a tone appropriate to an individual trying to find her unique identity, her blackness, in the homogeneous late-twentieth-century American culture. Too, the lower-case first-person pronoun emphasizes the speaker's diminished sense of self, which can be

enlarged only after she has accepted herself for what she is (as the poet suggests to the speaker).

5. Birth is literally a painful process, of course. The speaker is pointing up the fact that there are figurative births as well, such as the birth of a new identity as a result of an enlarging consciousness of self, and that these figurative births are also painful. The speaker is experiencing the birth of a new identity for herself; at the same time, an entire group of people, black Americans, is experiencing the birth of a new identity.

Anonymous

SIR PATRICK SPENS

1. The poem's attitude toward the king and the Scots lords is one
   of contempt, as the diction makes clear. They are seen as will-
   ful, unthinking men, dandies who fear to get their shoes wet.
   By the end of the poem, they are in their rightful place, at
   the feet of the noble ship's captain.

2. Sir Patrick Spens is a nobleman in every sense of the word. He
   respects the king's position and authority, if not the man himself, and thus does not even consider disobeying an order.

3. At the end of the poem, the true nobleman, Sir Patrick, is recognized by the poet as being superior to the lords. He has done
   his duty although he knew that carrying out his orders meant
   certain death.

Imamu Amiri Baraka (LeRoi Jones)

A POEM FOR BLACK HEARTS

1. Malcolm X, born in 1925, was an extremely influential leader in
   the black nationalist movement and a member of the Nation of
   Islam until he broke away to form his own Muslim sect in 1964.
   He was assassinated in 1965. Malcolm clearly saw black people—
   and wanted them to see themselves—as strong and dignified.

2. Malcolm had a piercing intelligence; he promised deliverance;
   he was forceful and worked unflaggingly for a greater social
   good.

3. His words were "the victor's tireless/thrusts," a fitting image
   for a brilliantly provacative orator.

POETRY

Robert Browning

LOVE AMONG THE RUINS

1. As the glories of the past are contrasted with the "quiet-colored" present, we are prepared for the final stanza of the poem in which the martial might of the ancients is revealed as frenetic folly, wasteful, transient, and sad.

2. The ruins are at once romantic and melancholy in their relation to the past. They bring to the present, though, anticipation and love.

3. History and the past contrast with the present, full of life and love.

William Cullen Bryant

THANATOPSIS

1. According to the poem, death brings about the loss of individual being while the physical body's elements return to the earth.

2. The poem seems to say that at least there is peace after death. Further, the person about to die should be consoled by the fact that he or she is about to join "the powerful of the earth—the wise, the good,/Fair forms, and hoary seers of ages past."

3. Nature here is seen as the great tomb of the dead, drawing its life from the dead and thus providing the continuity necessary for the world's survival.

John Donne

DEATH BE NOT PROUD

1. Death is dependent upon fate, chance, kings, desperate men, poison, war, and sickness—the agents or causes of death. Thus death's very existence is brought about by mishaps, microbes, and human beings.

2. Rest and sleep—like death, in Donne's mind, temporary states—can be brought with sleeping potions. Since we wake from death into eternal life, just as we awaken in the morning from our night's rest, death holds no more power over us than does a short nap.

3. The fact of eternal life makes death impotent.

H.D. (Hilda Doolittle)

EVENING

1. The fading light makes one ridge (of a valley or the garden) appear lighter than another; then one flower appears lighter, one darker; as the light fades, the hepatica petals turn inward and close, disappearing altogether in the dimness. The white buds on the small cornel tree(s) are visible to the end of the poem, but the shadows obliterate the roots, branches, and leaves, and the shadows that the branches and leaves had cast disappear in the general darkness.

2. Hepatica is an early perennial wildflower about six inches high with lustrous blue, lavendar, pink, or white flowers, often an inch across, that close at night. It is an appropriate choice for this poem since it is attractive, delicate, and responds visibly to the fading light. The hepaticas in the poem are blue, perhaps suggesting the sky.

   Cornel, a shrub or tree from the dogwood family, is a delicate, striking, almost leafless plant at home near the edge of a wood. Its blossoms stand out like stars against the darker background. The buds in this poem remind one of the stars, visible after all else has been lost, and they place the poem in the early spring, as do the hepaticas.

Thomas Gray

ODE ON THE DEATH OF A FAVORITE CAT, DROWNED IN A TUB OF GOLDFISHES

1. Gray uses these words to make an insignificant event more plausible and dramatic, with the point that trivial events are often given an importance they do not deserve.

2. Colors: azure flowers on the vase (3); snowy beard on the cat (8); her ears of jet and emerald eyes (11); Tyrian hue (16), richest purple (17), and golden gleam (18) of the goldfish; and gold (23, 42). The colors essentially cease after line 18, at which point the plot thickens as Selima is tempted by the fish and drowns. The colors thus appear to represent the pre-crisis state of tranquility in which we first view the tabby, a tacit allusion to the state of Adam and Eve before the Temptation and Fall.

3. Lofty, dignified elements include the following: calling the poem an ode, traditionally an exalted, dignified form; using the word lofty in the first line; employing serious diction throughout (e.g., blow, 3, for bloom, demurest, 4, for reserved, and so on); using unusual syntax, an apparent imitation of Milton and suggesting classical poets (e.g., "Her conscious tail her joy declared," 7, rather than "declared her joy"; or "The slippery verge her feet beguiled," 29, rather than "beguiled her feet"); maintaining a serious tone throughout (never does

the speaker wink at the incident as a ludicrous scene); citing
Fate (28), the gods of the sea and of streams (32), and sea
nymphs (34), as in serious, classical poems on death.

4. The speaker's attitude is expressed in line 23, "What female
heart can gold despise?" The final stanza reiterates the moral,
offered specifically to female readers ("ye beauties," 37).
Implicit, however, is the inclusion of males in this tale. With
"What cat's averse to fish?" (24), female or male, we are given
a hint that had the cat been male, he would have jumped in and
drowned just like Selima, grasping for "all that glisters" (42).

Thomas Hardy

THE CONVERGENCE OF THE TWAIN

1. The worms ignore the rich trappings and ornamental furnishings
of the great ship's salons.

2. By the collision it arranges, Immanent Will shapes the destinies
of the thousands of people affected.

3. Both are necessary to the collision.

George Herbert

EASTER-WINGS

1. The speaker reviews the biblical story of man's fall from grace
and of Christ's subsequent redemption of man from original sin
(accomplished at the season later called Easter by Christians).
In the second stanza he turns to his own sins, caused in part by
being born into a fallen world (11), and he finishes with the
request—similar to that in the first stanza—that Christ accept
him as a candidate for salvation (or speaking figuratively, to
enable him to fly above the fallen world and eventually into the
distant heavens). Underlying the poem's message is the paradox
of the fortunate fall: that the redemption (necessitated by
the fall) enables man to rise higher through the agency of
Christ than he would have risen, unaided, prior to the fall
(without having sinned).

2. This shaped poem correlates form and meaning in many ways. One
can locate visual reinforcement of the theme in such lines as
5 and 15: "most poor" and "most thin," the shortness of the
lines reiterating their meaning; or in the shrinking of the
line length as the speaker describes the decaying (3) or sick-
nesses and punishment of his soul (12, 13), and in the corresponding amplification of line length as he revives, through
Christ's help, and ascends.

94

The original printing of this poem in 1633 placed the two stanzas on separate and facing pages, presumably to represent the
wings of the lark and the book spine its body. Moreover, the
stanzas were printed upright, with the lines vertical rather
than horizontal as in most modern versions (including this one);
thus, the reader was obliged to turn the volume sideways to read
the lines. As a consequence, the original version effectively
draws the eyes downward toward the bottom of the pages as the
lines discuss decay, sin, sickness, and shame, and upward as
they refer to harmony, victory, and flight (or ascension to
heaven).

3. In Christian theology, sin causes spiritual deterioration. The
   lark in the poem represents the soul, whose decay—likened to
   the bird's damaged wing—must be repaired before it can ascend
   to God. Christ's atonement corrects the damaged wings of those
   who seek it, are worthy of it (through repentance), and accept
   it.

Gerard Manley Hopkins

GOD'S GRANDEUR

1. God's presence in the world, according to the poem, will manifest itself suddenly, flashing into our consciousness like the
   glint from the movement of metal foil in the sunlight (or from
   the length of bright steel in a fencing sword). Alternatively,
   this manifestation will dawn on us slowly, little by little, as
   oil is slowly pressed from olives and is collected in a gradually filling receptacle.

2. Alliteration is used, for example, in line 2; assonance is em-
   ployed as well, as in line 11. Internal rhyme, as in line 6,
   is another of the poem's sound devices, as is external rhyme.

3. The "black West" is opposed by morning in the East; sensitivity
   to nature is opposed by insensitivity; recognition of God is
   opposed by ignorance of Him.

A. E. Housman

TO AN ATHLETE DYING YOUNG

1. The home to which the athlete is carried is his last one, the
   grave.

2. After the athlete's death, silence means no more to him, according to the poem, than cheers would. The poem comments on the
   transitory nature of human accolades and earthly honors.

3. The name, at times, dies before the man in the sense that fame is fleeting. Even while a person lives, he or she may be forgotten by the very crowds that cheered a short time before.

Langston Hughes

I, TOO, SING AMERICA

1. The speaker is the "darker brother" and, by extension, all black Americans.

2. The controlling metaphor is the "black sheep of the family," the family mamber who is not appreciated but who in the end everyone is proud of.

3. The rest of the family, Americans who are not black, will be ashamed in the end for the way they have treated their brother.

Randall Jarrell

THE MOCKINGBIRD

1. "For a minute, in the moonlight" (20), the speaker is unable to discern the difference between reality and deception. At night, the mockingbird imitates various birds and a cat that were present during the day, and because these imitations are so realistic, the moonlight so sunlike, the speaker realizes how easily the senses are deceived.

2. Only at night and by moonlight is the bird able to sway the speaker, and then only "for a minute." In the absence of clear visual reinforcement, the other senses are more easily deceived. Also, the imagery may imply that people are more easily deceived when they are ignorant (in darkness) than when they can see clearly.

Elizabeth Jennings

IN MEMORY OF ANYONE UNKNOWN TO ME

1. A number of beliefs could give rise to this kind of non-specific grief: a humanistic belief in the similarity of all people: we don't have to know others personally to know the details of their suffering; an empathy created by imagining ourselves dying alone; an anger at the human condition of which death is a part.

2. "Sentiment" can denote an excessive, insincere emotion and in this sense is not a necessary part of grief. Most people, however, do believe that grief should have some emotional component.

3. The speaker's grief is pure in a classical sense--uncluttered by
   messy emotions, cleanly rational. But this grief's "purity"
   should probably not be read as "perfection"; it does seem rather
   unappealing in its coldness and austerity.

John Keats

TO AUTUMN

1. The images refer to twilight and hence are appropriate to a poem
   about autumn, the twilight of the year (as autumn closes out the
   cycle of the growing season, twilight closes out the hours of
   daylight). Indeed, the poem moves from dawn to dusk and from
   spring to autumn, in each case laying emphasis on the fall's
   particular significances and beauties.

2. Some students might say personification; others might say synecdoche. In either case, Keats clearly represents the season by
   selecting as its salient features activities—winnowing, cider-
   making—in which humans are involved during the season.

3. The image of the gathering swallows certainly reinforces the
   twilight tone and mood of the closing stanza as the tone and
   mood which the poet finds most appropriate to the season. On
   the other hand, we cannot be reminded of swallows and the fall
   without recalling the swallows' southern migrations in anticipation of the coming winter; and we are further reminded that
   one of the most familiar harbingers of spring is the return of
   the swallows to northern climes. By closing with that particular image, consequently, Keats leaves his reader with a vivid
   emblem of the cyclical processes of nature wherein each ending
   (autumn, twilight) signals a new beginning (spring, dawn).

John Keats

ODE ON A GRECIAN URN

1. There is, first of all, the often noted ambiguity of the word
   still: the urn is motionless; the urn has remained unravished.
   A further ambiguity lies in unravish'd: the urn has not been
   decayed by time or damaged; like the figures depicted on it, it
   is forever in its first flush of fulfillment. Finally, the urn
   is wedded to its own stillness and to the peaceful lives which
   it depicts. Students should have less difficulty determining
   how the urn is a "sylvan historian," though they might have to
   be introduced to the meaning of the adjective.

2. Keats calls our attention to those depictions on the urn that
   are related to youth, love, and beauty—in other words, that
   call to mind peacefulness and joy, a pastoral bliss.
   It is because the urn celebrates the joys of youth and a summery
   frolicsomeness that it pleases and inspires us to contemplate

perfection. Since it is also, however, a lifeless object, its
representation of eternal bliss is a cold one, void of the heat
of living passions: hence, "cold pastoral."

3. Students will very likely cite the third stanza as the one that
most points up the contrasts between the lives of the figures on
the urn and our own lives. Lines 15 to 20 in stanza two serve
as well. In either case, the essential contrast is between that
which is forever poised on the brink of blissful fulfillment—
the figures on the urn—and that which experiences joys after
joys but can never prevent a single moment from fading—ourselves. The figures on the urn have our passions; they do not
have our transiency.

Shirley Geok-Lin Lim

MODERN SECRETS

1. The dream shrinking "to its fiction" and "its end" and the sal-
low child are all described in some of the poem's shortest lines
(7-11). The shrinking (7) results in the poem's shortest (or
shrunk) line (8). In retelling the dream to us (lines 1-2, 11-
14), the speaker uses long lines, a burgeoning of the imagination in contrast to the shrinking of the dream to its fiction as
it is told to a friend (4). In addition, the lines create something of a shaped poem, a bowl-like curve (except for line 6),
perhaps representing the rice-bowl (12); the shape is bordered
conspicuously on each rim by the only two references to the
speaker's homeland.

2. The dream is never described; we know only that it was in Chinese (1). The speaker's point is that she or he is still tied,
from childhood, to China; that despite cultural adaptation to
the English-speaking western world, the speaker will always be
culturally part Chinese. This is the part that "hides in the
cupboard / With the tea-leaves and china" (13-14). The title
tells us that the poem reveals a secret, ostensibly that when a
child is transplanted to a foreign country, that child will
have dual identities even though she or he may seem to be
completely naturalized.

Archibald MacLeish

ARS POETICA

1. Students should have little difficulty in identifying the similes of lines 1-10, since they are object to object. Thus, a
poem is like a globed fruit, old medallion, casement stone, the
flight of birds, and a rising moon. As the poem continues, however, it is compared more and more to actions: moonlight moving
across branches, moonlight seen through bare branches, etc.
Students who follow that progression should begin to notice that

MacLeish is comparing the poem more to process and effect than to product and conclusion, and that MacLeish is also calling our senses rather than our minds into play. In both cases, the similes serve to underscore the central assertion that a poem should not mean but be; that is to say, a poem's appeal is to our sense of life's rhythms, textures, sounds, and tastes, not to our philosophical selves.

2. MacLeish no doubt intends meaning with that famous statement in "Ars Poetica"; yet there is the paradox that the meaning he intends is undermined by the very assertion itself. Naturally, we can forgive the poet; we can understand how he must make a statement of his own in order to free us from the common misconception that poetry is prettified philosophy. Equally paradoxical, of course, is the earlier assertion that a poem "should be equal to:/Not true." A clever student might see, however, that "not true" does not itself necessarily equal a lie. MacLeish is really saying that questions of true and not true, of truth and falsehood, should have no place in our consideration of poetic statement. In that sense, and in that sense only, a poem should not mean but be; i.e., meaning is secondary to execution.

3. Again, the paradox which "Ars Poetica" creates is that, if we believe what the poem says, then we should not believe the poem. After all, it tells us that poetry is the same as "not true" and that poetry should not mean but be; at one end, we are led to believe that it lies; but if it lies, then perhaps a poem should mean and not be. Those sorts of conundrums, more often used by philosophers to illustrate the limits of logic, are themselves illustrative of MacLeish's meaning, however; for what he does seem to be saying is that confusion and perplexity are the only results of approaching poetry as if it were logical discourse.

YOU, ANDREW MARVELL

1. The poem traces the course of the development of civilization in the West from its foundations in the Tigris and Euphrates valley to the more recent centers founded by the Moors and by the Spaniards in Western Europe. Thus it is tracing the course of empire and emphasizing, with subtlety, its transient nature.

2. It is reasonable to assume that the speaker is located in the American heartland, the Midwest. Once we know where the speaker is, we realize that the poem suggests that America is having its own moment in the sun now, but that our own halcyon days will likewise eventually slip into the night that is past history.

3. The poem has meaning; we cannot deny that, even if we might dispute what that meaning is. Since "Ars Poetica" asks poetry to appeal first and foremost to our senses, however, we must admit that "You, Andrew Marvell" achieves that aim and that we assign it its meaning.

John Milton

WHEN I CONSIDER HOW MY LIGHT IS SPENT

1. Despite the prevailing critical attitude that the poem addresses itself to Milton's blindness, encourage your students to come up with other interpretations for the speaker's "light"—for example, intellectual acumen, spiritual acuity, creative inspiration.

2. The speaker is rescued from despair by his realization that there are myriad ways in which to serve, and hence that he is far from finished with his earthly tasks. Such a conclusion can be sustained within a theocentric as well as a wholly secular framework. That Milton works within a spiritual context should not preclude discussion of the poem as its theme relates to any number of different pursuits and aspirations.

3. In the most general terms, the line can be interpreted to mean that those who serve must serve as God desires, even if that service is simply to be ready and waiting at hand. To chaff against a service that does not seem to be what one expected is, after all, not to be of service. Milton sees both the will and the wisdom of any one individual as totally inferior and subservient to the will and the wisdom of God. The individual, in Milton's view, consequently finds his or her true peace in trusting in God's will, no matter what.

Sylvia Plath

LADY LAZARUS

1. The speaker is a woman who narrowly escaped death when she was ten ("It was an accident"), who tried to kill herself when she was twenty, and who now, at thirty, wants to die again.

2. The images of oppression ("Nazi lampshade," "O my enemy," "The peanut-crunching crowd/Shoves in to see," "I am your valuable/ The pure gold baby") suggest that the speaker feels brutalized, driven to suicide by something implacable. The means of death are variously shown as butchery, decomposition, and cremation; the oppressor(s) appear to be male ("Herr Doktor," "Herr Enemy").

3. Lazarus was a Jew, a fitting protagonist in a poem about victimization, especially given the Teutonic images here. Also, the situation of Lazarus's death provided Jesus an opportunity to show the power and mercy of God in raising him to life; the speaker in Plath's poem is called forth from death like Lazarus, but not in the spirit of love: ironically, her saviors are exploitative ("There is a charge/For the eyeing of my scars") and unfeeling ("the same brute/Amused shout").

OTHER POEMS TO READ

4. The poem is of the self-confessional mode and deals squarely
   with psychic pain, rejecting easy relief and promising a kind of
   revenge for past injustices.

Edgar Allen Poe

THE RAVEN

1. Poe's speaker has been driven to distraction by his grief over
   the death of his beloved Lenore. That grief has so deranged his
   sense of proportion and reality that he will grasp at any
   straw—including the appearance of the raven—in his attempt to
   come to grips with the irrevocable loss of Lenore, a loss which
   he nevertheless assumes is not a permanent one.

2. The appearance of a raven in the speaker's study is, of course,
   the most prominent detail among the devices which Poe uses to
   give the poem its haunting mood. That the speaker has been
   studying ancient and perhaps forbidden texts is another element,
   causing us to wonder why he may have been studying them. Was
   he, for example, about to conduct a ceremony in black magic to
   call up Lenore's ghost from the land of the dead? It is, after
   all, midnight, the witching hour. A further feature of Poe's
   mood-creating devices is the speaker's temperament as that comes
   through in his language: he is easily excitable and clearly not
   rational; the feverish nature of his excitement and irrational-
   ity overwhelm us as we read (as do the tom-tom beat and monotonous rhyme scheme). We are confronted with a favorite characterization of Poe's, the obsessive personality.

3. The single dramatic effect is one that may have to be called to
   your students' attention but one that they will not dispute once
   it is pointed out to them—the fact that the raven has apparently been taught to speak only one word, "Nevermore," and yet it
   answers the speaker's questions each time, making him more and
   more distracted as the poem continues. You might wish to share
   with your students Poe's own comments on the poem in his "Essay
   on Composition."

Ezra Pound

BALLAD OF THE GOODLY FERE

1. Pound is imagining what Simon Zelotes, a man of the people,
   would have sounded like if ordinary seventeenth-century English
   had been spoken in Palestine at the time of Christ. Clearly,
   he would have spoken not the king's English but a more colorful,
   earthy English, and that is the style of speech which Pound
   tries to approximate. In the same manner, Pound used the ballad
   form because it was the most popular format for the street
   poetry of Jacobean England. Simon would have spoken like a
   working-man rather than a scholar and a gentleman, and if he

had chosen to tell his story, he would have used a form of poetry familiar to the Londoner and one created as much for purposes of recitation as for reading.

2. The irony in stanza six is that, as every student knows, they did get Jesus "in a book"; the Jesus whom Simon claims to know, a man of the people like himself, is the last Jesus many of us think of, for the very reason that there are yards of Scripture and scholarship between any one individual and the living Christ. Pound is being anti-clerical, anti-intellectual, and perhaps even anti-religious through his persona, but he is not being anti-Christ.

3. Simon is made to confirm Christ's resurrection in the truncated final stanza. Once the reader knows that Simon is speaking after having witnessed the resurrected Christ, it should give Simon's words, and Pound's intentions, all that much more clarity and strength.

Edward Arlington Robinson

RICHARD CORY

1. The poem works by the suddenness with which Cory's suicide is revealed to us, and Robinson achieves that effect by not giving us the slightest clue that that event will have occurred by poem's end. A student might say that he or she had suspected as much, but that would be on the basis of intuition, not of any information provided in the poem.

2. The speaker envies Cory for his wealth, station, physical beauty, and apparent contentment. On a second reading, however, some students might see behind the envy a certain admiration—indeed, the only verse that suggests envy is line 12. Cory is for the speaker and his or her fellow townsfolk some evidence of the perfection that the human can achieve, and it is that fact which makes his sudden suicide all the more tragically poignant an event. Obviously, the details of his inner life are missing from the poem.

3. The poem is an illustration of the aphorism that the grass is always greener on the other side of the fence. Robinson effectively reminds us that we should try always to put ourselves in the other person's shoes before jumping to conclusions about whether that person's life is better or worse than our own. In other words, each person has his own problems. By allowing us to form this conclusion for ourselves rather than presenting us with it as the poem's moral, Robinson shows his respect both for our intelligence and for the fact that poetry is art, not philosophy or sermonizing.

OTHER POEMS TO READ

Muriel Rukeyser

BOY WITH HIS HAIR CUT SHORT

1. One of the purposes of this moving poem is to communicate the
   feelings shared by most people in trying to make their way in
   the world, in finding their first full-time job, in seeking em-
   ployment in a large and unfriendly city. The poem is effective
   in communicating a poignancy in this universal endeavor. For
   example, we are allowed to perceive the sister's lack of confidence in her young brother's chances, and we suspect that he
   too sees this in her gaze (23). The brother and sister, piti-
   able figures against the impersonal city, elicit our sympathy.

2. His neck is _exposed_ (6), implying that he is too naive, trusting, and gullible to succeed in the sophisticated and decadent
   city; his eye _blears_ (8) as he looks far to the side, implying
   that he has shed childish tears at his failure; his forehead
   appears to be a _child's_ (13) or that of an adolescent (20), a
   physical suggestion of his immaturity, as is _the fine hair_ (17);
   "he lets his head fall" (22), a motion of defeat; his sister's
   look is _hopeless_ (23), the room is _darkened_ and the red neon
   sign _impersonal_ (24). All these point repeatedly to defeat.

3. The neon arrow impresses the boy because of its precision in
   always reaching its mark (11, 12). One comes away with the
   distinct impression that the arrow sign is included because it
   knows where to go at each flash, that it is secure in its activity, and is directed. In contrast, the boy appears nearly
   directionless, having searched without success for weeks (16)
   and having seemingly no idea where to look further.

Norman H. Russell

INDIAN SCHOOL

1. The speaker, reflecting a native American point of view, finds
   the world of his white brother an alien one: he finds nothing
   to admire, yet he reflects no hatred. Rather, he admits his
   inability "to know / gods purpose in him" (21-22), and displays
   a marked fear of the white man and his environment (he is
   frightened, 3, at the strangeness of the house, and he compares
   the white man to a wounded bear, 15, perhaps dying but still
   dangerous).

2. Russell's speaker is puzzled, intimidated, and repulsed by his
   white brother; Welch's is cynical and bitter at the diseases,
   broken promises, and the "far corner of a flat world" (3) given
   to these people by the whites. Both speakers view their white
   brothers as grotesque: "in his odd robes / uglier / than any
   other creature i have ever seen" (Russell, lines 18-20); "a
   slouching dwarf with rainwater eyes" (Welch, 7).

103

3. A possible explanation is the speaker's low opinion of the
   school and of the whole white environment, not worthy of being
   dignified by capitalization. The lower-case technique also represents rebellion against convention, and the lower-case "i"
   might be interpreted as the speaker's feelings about self while
   in the house and the school—a loss of esteem and self-worth.

Anne Sexton

LAMENT

1. In both poems, trees are endowed with human sensitivity, and the
   only animal included (excluding the goose in "Lament," 20) is
   the cat; both involve the death of a person (in Sexton's, the
   death has already occurred; in Levertov's, it is about to occur); both focus on prevention of the death, Sexton's a lament
   that the speaker failed to prevent it, Levertov's a building of
   suspense regarding whether the peppertree will (and can) prevent
   it.

2. The speaker seems to be female ("The supper dishes are over,"
   26), but this identity is not clear. The person is an adult
   (knows what lewdness is, 3, and reflects the contemplative viewpoint of an adult, probably over thirty). The verbal facility
   of the poem attests to the speaker's intelligence and probable
   education. Confessions of inaction suggest a person of little
   assertiveness or courage; furthermore, the speaker is not calm
   under stress (13).

3. The someone appears to have died in an automobile accident (8-
   9), but this is not entirely clear. The speaker apparently was
   present in one of the vehicles involved (note the chance, not
   taken, to notice "the neck of the driver," 8); the speaker la-
   ments that she was not "firm as a nurse" (7), apparently about
   aspects of the drive; and the following lines might well refer
   to a hospital emergency room: "I think I could have charmed the
   table, / the stained dish or the hand of the dealer" (14-15).
   Evidence for a firm interpretation, however, is thin.

William Shakespeare

SONNET 18

1. As the speaker very clearly tells us, he will not compare his
   beloved to a summer's day because even something as superfi-
   cially ideal as such a day becomes, on closer examination,
   filled with blemishes and imperfections. In the speaker's eyes,
   his beloved has no blemishes or imperfection; hence, the
   speaker will not compare his beloved to a summer's day which is
   less lovely, less temperate, and less likely to remain itself
   for very long.

2. A paraphrase of the seventh line of the poem would be rendered
as follows: everything that is beautiful sooner or later becomes less and less beautiful until, in time, it is no longer
beautiful at all. Despite his acceding to that truism, the
speaker nevertheless believes that his beloved's beauty will
never fade because he has preserved its essence in his poem.
The poet's words thus are a portrait of the beloved's loveliness, for they convey to readers the power of the love that such
loveliness inspired in the poet. We can only imagine what the
beloved must actually have looked like; still, we are convinced
by the poet's praise and ardor that she must certainly have
been beautiful. Consequently, "thy eternal summer shall not
fade . . . when in eternal lines to time thou growest"; the
poet has immortalized her beauty in this poem.

William Shakespeare

SONNET 60

1. The initial simile is a remarkably apt description of the passage of time: the peak of each wave representing individual
seconds (or minutes, 2), and the continuous, fluid motion of
the ocean moving these peaks toward the shore signifying the
smooth and inexorable advancement of time. The "pebbled shore"
(1) represents the present moment. The standard meter in
Shakespeare's sonnets, iambic pentameter, here functions as a
rhythmic reinforcement of the waves breaking on the shore.
Moreover, if the final rhymed couplet is omitted, the remaining
twelve lines and their sixty iambic feet might be viewed as a
structural and rhythmic representation of the seconds in a
minute, the minutes in an hour, the hours in a day, the months
in a year—or in short, the cycles of time. Although Shakespeare, as far as we know, did not assign the present numbers to
his 154 published sonnets, printed as they were without his
supervision, the aptness of this sonnet's number (and that of
Sonnet 12, another sonnet that refers directly to the cycles of
time) is plain.

2. Time is the villain. It destroys all living things. The sea,
especially in Shakespeare's day when shipwreck was common, is
also an enemy to humanity. Both time and the sea are uncon-
trollable: humans cannot prevent time's passing, nor can they
(even today) exert much control over the movements and forces of
the oceans.

3. The stages of human life: infancy (5-6), during which the child
is the center of attention (and self-centered); maturity (6-7),
during which the adult achieves success (crown'd), yet must
fight ill fortune; and age (8), during which time, once man's
benefactor, now leads him toward dissolution. The only hope
extended to the person addressed is the perpetuation of his
or her memory through being the subject of the present sonnet.

4. This question calls for a personal answer.

James Welch

THE MAN FROM WASHINGTON

1. The speaker is saying that the white races who dispossessed the
   native Americans brought them materialism, empty promises, and
   "fabulous disease" (13).

2. The representative of Washington (and by extension, all white
   people) is in actuality a puny physical specimen. His appearance thus contrasts with a stereotyped image of a native American primitive man: tall, powerful, vigorous, and undefiled.
   The dwarf comes down because he is condescending to the Indians;
   he slouches probably because he is not well, either physically,
   mentally, morally, or spiritually—a depiction similar to those
   in Norman H. Russell's "indian school," of the white man as
   "the staggering old bear / filled with many arrows" (15-16), and
   in Wendy Rose's "For the White Poets Who Would Be Indian" (both
   in this chapter). The eyes of Welch's dwarf also give him away:
   he has no compassion, no vigor, no life.

3. Because the native Americans are promised inoculations against
   promise (13), one must suppose that this means they are to be
   rendered immune to the promises made to them but (according to
   history) often broken; in short, that any promises made will not
   be kept, yet because of their inoculations they will not suffer
   from these breaches. The irony is that the protective inoculations are themselves merely a promise.

Walt Whitman

WHEN I HEARD THE LEARN'D ASTRONOMER

1. Whitman is expressing a common gripe against the scientist's
   fascination with facts and figures, and that is that all the
   facts and figures still do not add up to the whole effect of a
   particular phenomenon of nature upon the sensitive soul. Thus,
   the speaker is made "tired and sick," but, being a modern man in
   a rational culture, he seems to be apologizing for his inability
   to work up any enthusiasm for the astronomer's charts. On
   closer examination, however, some students might see a certain
   irony in that unaccountable; it is not so much that the speaker
   cannot account for this lack of interest in science as that he
   feels that there are events and objects in the natural universe
   which cannot be weighed and measured—counted—without missing
   the point. Finally, then, the poem is an attack on the analy-
   tical person who counts and measures but never comes to any
   sense of appreciation or wonder in the face of the whole, of
   the synthesis that is the thing itself.

2. Clearly, the speaker was most upset by the mathematical precision of the astronomer's presentation, that is, by his cut-and-
   dried attention to the "facts," as if they were all that mat-
   tered. The others in the audience seem to have been impressed—

"with much applause"—but the speaker gets away from both the astronomer's lecture and the audience's enthusiasm by going out to look at the stars themselves "in perfect silence."

3. The stars make no attempt to explain themselves; they simply are. The speaker wants to be able to share that fact with them rather than have his head stuffed with the astronomer's great quantity of facts about them. He does not feel that many others share his attitude; he goes off by himself, apparently purposefully seeking solitude, and talks of the mystical night air in which he can experience and share in the wholeness of the universe rather than its separate and subdivided parts.

DRAMA

CHAPTER 16   PLOT

Sophocles

OEDIPUS THE KING

1. The prologue sets the scene, establishes the position of Oedipus and Apollo, introduces the conflict, and reveals Oedipus's
   intent to deal with it. The next four scenes comprise the four
   main episodes of the drama in which Oedipus encounters his four
   antagonists. Each confrontation brings him closer to the
   truth. In Scene One Oedipus insults Teiresias, whose prophe-
   cies and accusations he rejects. In Scene Two Oedipus shows
   his temper and accuses Creon of treason. In Scene Three Oedipus unleashes his anger on the messenger, whom he questions
   about his parentage, and shifts his attention from searching
   for the murderer of Laius to discovering his own true identity.
   In Scene Four he again displays his fury, striking the shepherd
   who reveals his identity. Finally, the Exodos completes the
   action of the play: Jocasta hangs herself and Oedipus blinds
   himself.

2. The prologue frams the action of the drama, sets the tone, reveals the character of Oedipus, establishes the importance of
   Apollo, introduces the conflict, and emphasizes the dramatic
   irony of the situation.

3. The chorus performs as the "voice" of another character, pro-
   jecting the views and emotions of the Theban citizens. The
   chorus also re-examines the past, explains character, prepares
   the spectators for subsequent action, and comments on significant moral issues.

4. That moment in which Oedipus moves from ignorance to knowledge
   about his true identity is the most dramatic moment of his
   life.

5. Oedipus has been a good ruler, showing concern and sorrow for
   the plight of his people and compassion for his daughters. He
   shows that he is quick to act when, early in the drama, he vows
   to seek Laius's murderer and rid the city of its pestilence and
   when, later, he punishes himself and demands his own exile.
   Throughout the play, Oedipus demonstrates his courage and commitment to the truth.

6. Vanity, pride, and a reckless temper lead Oedipus to the murder of Laius and to his eventual fall.

7. a. Oedipus makes the very choices that contribute to his fall.
   b. The oracles have determined his fate. Any attempt to escape this truth is futile.

8. They are indeed appropriate. "Swollen foot" may suggest a human flaw such as swollen pride in the character of Oedipus. "On the track of knowledge" parallels his movement from blindness toward perception.

9. Teiresius, the blind prophet/priest of Apollo, knows the truth about Oedipus's parentage and crimes. Later, as he knows the truth, Oedipus's enlightenment and self-inflicted blindness make him a Teiresias-figure. Creon, a wise, reasonable man, exhibits the gentleness and restraint that Oedipus lacks. In the prologue Creon wants his news delivered privately, and in the Exodos he wants to minimize public grief. By contrast, Oedipus wants to bring everything into the open.

10. Possible themes include the following: Do not count anyone happy who has not yet completed his life; or, what the gods decree, a mortal cannot change.

George Bernard Shaw

ARMS AND THE MAN

1. Finding refuge in Raina's bedroom, Bluntschli is attracted to Raina, a romantic heroine. Sergius, an ideal hero, pledged to Raina, becomes enamored of the defiant servant girl, Louka. Louka rejects Nicola, the servant, and wins Sergius away from Raina. A lovesick Bluntschli returns to claim Raina.

2. Shaw introduces several major characters, explains details of background and character, establishes the play as comedy by aiming his satirical gun at the business of war, and creates excitement and suspense.

3. Shaw's primary concern is with ideas. He is intent on showing the idiocy of war, the foolishness of romantic ideals, and the imprudence of human pretensions and servant-class morality.

4. Bluntschli is the protagonist. He is efficient, unemotional, and master of every situation in which he is involved. He is a realist in control. Bluntschli is Shaw's vehicle for satirizing society and the romantic illusions of love and war.

5. During the course of the play Raina changes from being a romantic to being a realist, thanks to Bluntschli's influence.

6. Comedy is composed of incongruity, and Shaw makes ample use of the unexpected to get us to laugh at war, romance, pretensions,

honor, morality, social status, politics, and other aspects of society. Some examples of the smaller comic devices Shaw uses would be Bluntschli's ironic understatements (Raina: "If Sergius knew, he would challenge you and kill you in a duel." Bluntschli: "Bless me! then dont tell him."), some broad slapstick (the coat that suddenly appears in the blue closet); but most of the comedy is essential to the play, a part of its thematic integrity, as the characters discover the hollowness of their beliefs.

7. Shaw repudiates war as brutal, foul, and senseless. These views are made clear by the actions and speeches, primarily those of Bluntschli but also those of Major Petkoff and Sergius.

8. This question calls for personal responses from students.

Arthur Miller

DEATH OF A SALESMAN

1. Protagonist: Willy Loman

   Prize: success

   Obstacle: his pride

   Point of Attack: Biff finds his father with another woman

   Complications: all of Willy's failures at his job, getting
                   fired, his refusal to face reality, and the
                   false values he teaches his sons

   Climax: Biff lambasts Willy with the truth

   Resolution: Willy commits suicide

   Theme: materialistic values are hollow

2. Miller immediately gets our attention by having Linda ask, "What
   happened?" He creates suspense by not telling us anything more
   than Linda's next question, "You didn't smash the car, did you?"

3. Loman is a loud-mouthed little man who dreams of success, which
   he interprets in purely economic terms. He lives in the past
   and the future, never in the present. His dreams of material
   success have so dominated his thinking that he lives by a dis-
   torted sense of values, which he passes on to his sons. He ends
   up a total failure as a father, husband, businessman, and human
   being. His flaws are his pride, his inability to be honest with
   himself or with others, his obsession with success, and his
   failure to face reality. Nevertheless, we can sympathize with
   and pity Willy. Though his values and his approach are wrong
   and misdirected, he believes in them and holds on to his dreams
   for himself and his sons. He does the best he knows how. All
   his life he struggles for his family, even in suicide.

113

4. Biff and Happy are copies of the original. Their idea of success is money. We sympathize with the young men because they know no better than to think and act as their father taught them.

5. Linda is too quick to support and encourage Willy in all that he does.

6. Bernard is like the son Willy did not have; Charley is in charge of his destiny; Ben is a symbol of the success Willy might have had; Howard represents new, young management and success. Ben, Howard, and Charley, having achieved their dreams of success, serve as contrasts to Willy; Bernard functions as a contrast to Willy's sons.

7. They see Willy acting as a child, recognizing the fact that he has not yet grown up to accept his full responsibilities as a salesman, father, and husband.

8. Willy, the salesman, sold his boys a way of life based on falsehood and thus ruined their lives and his own life. The title refers both to his literal death and to the death of his false values. "Loman" seems to suggest low man on the ladder of success.

9. After Willy learns that Biff really loves him, he comes to realize that he alone must bear the responsibility for Biff's failure.

10. When Linda says, "We're free . . . We're free . . ." she refers to having made the last mortgage payment on the house. But beneath the surface the speech suggests release from all of Willy's undesirable influences.

Paddy Chayefsky

MARTY

1. In Act I the Italian woman and the young mother quickly introduce and repeat the topic of the play, asking Marty, "When you gonna get married?" The next scene shows Angie and Marty at a loss about what to do with themselves on a Saturday night (a perennial problem) and Marty's failure to make a date with Mary Feeney. The concluding action discusses the eviction of Aunt Catherine, whom Marty invites to move in with his mother and him. In Act II Marty faces immediate rejection by the first girl he asks to dance; he meets Clara Davis, with whom he dances; and he takes her home, introduces her to his mother, and makes a date with her for the following evening. In Act III Aunt Catherine again warns Marty's mother against the danger of being put out of her own house when Marty marries. Despite disapproval of Clara from Mother, Angie, and others, Marty decides to call his girl and take her to a movie.

2. Marty is the protagonist. He would like "a nice girl to marry" but lacks confidence in himself. These elements are brought together in the point of attack (introduction of the conflict), when Marty telephones Mary Feeney for a date and she turns him down.

3. The following are complications:

   a. Goaded on by Angie, Marty telephones Mary Feeney for a date but is rejected.

   b. Aunt Catherine, having caused a quarrel between Thomas (Marty's cousin) and his wife, is cast out of her house and invited to stay with Marty and his mother.

   c. At the Waverly Ballroom, Marty rejects a young man's offer to take someone else's date home.

   d. Aunt Catherine warns Marty's mother about her impending eviction when Marty marries.

   e. Clara Davis invites disapproval by saying that a mother-in-law should not live with a young couple.

   f. Mother finds fault with Clara.

4. As Aunt Catherine interfered with the lives of Thomas and Virginia, she disrupts the status quo in Marty's house. She creates a conflict between mother and son where none existed before. She is, she thinks, the prime example of what will happen to Marty's mother should Marty get married.

5. a. These characters are one-dimensional caricatures.

   b. Like Marty, they are lonely bachelors, interested in girls but not successful with them. Their presence heightens Marty's conflict.

6. Angie's dramatic function is, as Marty's closest friend, to shed light on Marty's motives. He represents what Marty was, and what he still would be without Clara Davis.

7. Virginia and Thomas provide an example of married life; their action causes Aunt Catherine to move in with Mother and Marty, which puts more pressure on Marty to find a girl.

8. a. Marty exhibits an easy-going manner and a generous heart.

   b. Marty demonstrates these traits consistently in rejecting the offer to take the "dog" home, in comforting Clara when she cries, and in continually trying to please his mother.

9. The play contains an abundance of such examples.

10. Not heeding the advice he receives from his mother and his friends, Marty, in his resolve to telephone Clara, settles his conflict.

Bertolt Brecht

THE CAUCASIAN CHALK CIRCLE

1. a. Brecht portrays the peasant class as exploited and corrupted
      by the ruling class and oppressed by the unjust economic
      system they control. Furthermore, the peasant class is made
      to suffer atrocity from the stupid wars the rulers instigate.

   b. The ruling class is characterized as stupid, cruel, and
      decadent.

2. The proverbs are the peasants' way of communicating indirectly
   and understanding their true feelings. They also confirm their
   folk heritage which is grounded in earthy, humorous wisdom.

3. The absurd story of Grusha's journey into the northern mountains
   is no less believable than the absurdities we have discovered
   about the wars of this century.

4. Both are victims of circumstances beyond their control, both
   perform acts of kindness to someone in need, both survive, and
   both change strikingly.

5. People who own anything are bad and people who own nothing are
   good.

August Strindberg

MISS JULIE

1. Julie is naive, weak, contradictory, and irrational. She does
   not know who she is or where she is going; she is unable to
   cope with reality; and she blames her father, her mother, and
   her ex-fiancé for her predicament.

2. a. Either Julie seeks happiness, as Strindberg suggests in the
      "Author's Foreword" to the play, or she is so thoroughly
      confused that she has no idea what she wants.

   b. In Strindberg's view there is no way that Julie can triumph.

3. The seduction scene, the plan to run away, and the Count's return are complications to Julie's search for love. The love scene brings Julie down to Jean's level; the escape cannot work since they have no money; and Julie must "face the music" or perish when the Count returns.

4. The father's faulty approach to Julie's upbringing, the mother's hatred of men, the fiancé's influence, the absence of the father, Julie's own weaknesses, and the influence of the festive atmosphere of a Midsummer Eve all contribute to Julie's downfall.

5. Jean is a coward because he fears Kristin, a liar when he tells Julie about hiding in the oats bin, and an opportunist when he makes love to Julie for self-aggrandizement and satisfaction.

6. Kristin is a "female slave" who lies, steals, and cheats. She hides behind the church and its moral precepts to expunge her sins. Her chief function is to expose a counterfeit society which lives by a double standard of morality.

7. The father is the authority figure for both Julie and Jean. Though never on stage, he affects the decisions and actions they take. The ringing of the bell (a call for service) expedites Julie's decision to kill herself.

8. The romantic is apt to believe that if Julie had found the "right person," she would have survived. Strindberg, who espouses the views of the naturalist, maintains that any person who "cannot come to terms with reality" must perish.

9. a. The seduction begins Julie's fall from a higher level to a lower level.

   b. The peasants' dance complements the atmosphere of romance.

   c. The greenfinch or canary is a symbol of Julie's childlike dreams and fantasies, to which she clings. They are destroyed when Jean chops its head off.

10. Strindberg implies that one social class is no better than another. Julie, an aristocrat, is as crude and lowly as the servant class which Jean and Kristin represent; and Jean at times acts with the taste and polish of higher society.

William Shakespeare

OTHELLO, THE MOOR OF VENICE

1. Protagonist: Othello

   Prize: acceptance

   Obstacle: his pride and gullibility

   Point of Attack: the announcement of Othello's marriage to
                     Desdemona

   Complications: the accusation that Othello used magic; Cassio's
                   fight with Roderigo and Montano; Desdemona's
                   attempts to get Cassio reinstated; Desdemona's
                   "tender" meeting with Cassio; the handkerchief
                   in Iago's possession, later given to Cassio;
                   Cassio's killing of Roderigo

   Climax: scene of Desdemona's murder

   Resolution: Emilia's finding out the truth about the handker-
                chief and Iago

   Theme: uncontrolled jealousy leads to self-destruction, or mal-
           icious hatred cannot triumph

2. a. Othello is a Moorish noble of royal lineage. He is proud,
      intelligent, strong-willed, self-disciplined, idealistic,
      gullible, inexperienced with women, and quick to judge.

   b. These traits are revealed by his speeches and inaction, and
      to a lesser degree by his actions and those of other charac-
      ters, especially Iago.

3. a. Early in the play Cassio, Desdemona, and Othello speak of
      Iago as an honest fellow. Later in the play Roderigo, after
      learning that he has been made a fool of by Iago, calls him
      an "inhuman dog." Emilia also discovers Iago to be false,
      as does Othello.

b. Iago is evil but wears the mask of goodness. He is a cynical egotist, a consummate conniver and deceiver.

4. Iago vows to turn Othello against Cassio and destroy "his peace and quiet and drive him to madness." When Iago admits to hating the Moor, early in the play, he begins to implement his vindictive plans.

5. Critics argue repeatedly about the plausibility of Iago's motives to destroy the Moor. Some hold that sufficient motivation is lacking and his behavior is inconsistent. Others find sufficient motivation by pointing to the fact that Iago is envious of Cassio's promotion to lieutenant, suspicious of his wife's fidelity (presuming she was having an affair with Othello), sexually attracted to Desdemona, and jealous of Othello's position and success.

6. Each of these characters serves an important role in the action of the play and contributes to the theme. Cassio functions as a loyal officer to Othello, whom he admires as a valiant man of honor. He is a character foil to Othello. Although a noble (and naive) Venetian lady, Desdemona deceives her father and lies to her husband. She serves as a character foil to Emilia. Roderigo's function is to keep Iago in money and perform his dirty tricks. Emilia speaks a language somewhat contradictory to her noble actions; she acts as a character foil to Desdemona.

7. Othello appears to be intelligent, strong-willed, even-tempered, and honorable, but is he? Iago deceives everyone into believing that he is the model of honesty and loyalty. Cassio is not as completely dependable as he seems to be. And Desdemona, while giving the impression of being naive and innocent, really is not.

8. Roderigo's love for Desdemona and Cassio's relationship with Bianca are two subplots intricately woven into the main action. They reveal character, advance the story, and amplify the theme.

9. a. Hardly credible, unless we believe that there is a little madness in everyone.

b. Othello naturally trusts Iago because he acts the part of a good, loyal friend. Iago expresses his love for the Moor, confides in him, and gives him no cause to distrust him.

c. To a rational, thinking person the handkerchief provides insufficient motivation for Othello's behavior, but to an irrational person the evidence may prove adequate.

d. Othello murders his wife because he is temporarily insane, or perhaps because he feels compelled to act as judge-executioner.

Edward Albee

THE SANDBOX

1. Albee depicts a world devoid of humanity and filled with absurdity. People do not care for one another. They exist in disharmony with themselves, other people, and their environment.

2. The Sandbox is "about" the human condition. Life is portrayed as sterile and empty and death is shown as void of dignity.

3. These characters show no affection for one another, display no emotion for anyone or anything, barely communicate, and have little to say of any importance.

4. a. Grandma is the only real person in the play. She understands other people, listens, and makes sense. She has, however, become disagreeable, cranky, and difficult because of the influence of her environment.

   b. The Young Man is handsome and friendly. His smile and friendly greeting are superficial. He does not know his name and forgets his lines. His role is that of the angel of death.

5. None of the characters in the play, except possibly Grandma, is concerned with anyone else. This fits Albee's purpose: to depict life as empty of humanity, substance, and value.

6. The unfurnished, destitute stage complements Albee's intention of showing the emptiness of life.

7. The dialogue is full of clichés, doubletalk, meaningless expressions, and empty pauses. The language, next to character, is Albee's chief means of showing us a world devoid of humanity.

8. The sandbox suggests Grandma's grave. But before she buries herself in it, it is a symbol of her childhood. She plays in it with a toy pail and shovel. The sandbox also serves to emphasize the emptiness of present civilization.

CHAPTER 20   OTHER PLAYS TO READ

Anton Chekhov

THE CHERRY ORCHARD

1. The play is a comedy chiefly because of the amusement we derive
   from the contradictions and absurdities we discover in the system of life the characters portray and the views they hold.

2. The cherry orchard is a reminder of lost happiness and a beautiful life once lived.

3. Lopahin's long speech in the opening scene with Dunyasha typi-
   fies Chekhov's dialogue. Speeches (monologues) are directed
   primarily at the audience as exposition rather than at another
   actor, and are spoken generally to benefit the speaker.

Henrik Ibsen

AN ENEMY OF THE PEOPLE

1. Protagonist: Dr. Stockman

   Antagonist: Peter Stockmann

   Conflict: between the two brothers, who must decide to do some-
              thing or nothing about the contaminated baths. Anoth-
              er real issue is the individual versus society.

2. Ibsen's drama seems to show that an individual, however right,
   cannot beat the majority or the system. The theme comes through
   the interplay of the characters.

3. Dr. Stockmann is vain, unworldly, idealistic, fond of creature
   comforts, and has difficulty controlling his temper. He believes in people and their wisdom to act for the common good
   and is proud of the power he thinks he has. Peter regards people with distrust but knows how to manage them by appealing to
   their self-interest. Unlike his brother, he is shrewd, wily,
   worldly, and realistic.